C000262762

Maths

Assessment Papers

11+-12+ years

Book 2

OXFORD

UNIVERSITY PRESS

OXFORD
UNIVERSITY PRESS

Great Clarendon Street, Oxford, OX2 6DP, United Kingdom

Oxford University Press is a department of the University of Oxford.
It furthers the University's objective of excellence in research, scholarship,
and education by publishing worldwide. Oxford is a registered trade mark of
Oxford University Press in the UK and in certain other countries

Text © David Clemson 2015

The moral rights of the authors have been asserted

First published in 2015

British Library Cataloguing in Publication Data
Data available

978-0-19-274019-9

10 9 8 7 6 5 4

Paper used in the production of this book is a natural, recyclable
product made from wood grown in sustainable forests.
The manufacturing process conforms to the environmental
regulations of the country of origin.

Printed in China

Acknowledgements

The publishers would like to thank the following for permissions to
use copyright material:

Page make-up: Tech-Set Ltd
Cover illustrations: Lo Cole

Although we have made every effort to trace and contact all
copyright holders before publication this has not been possible in all
cases. If notified, the publisher will rectify any errors or omissions at
the earliest opportunity.

Before you get started

What is Bond?

This book is part of the Bond Assessment Papers series for maths, which provides **thorough and continuous practice of all the key maths content** from ages five to thirteen. Bond's maths resources are ideal preparation for many different kinds of tests and exams – from SATs to 11+ and other secondary school selection exams.

How does the scope of this book match real exam content?

Maths 11+–12+ Book 1 and *Book 2* are the advanced Bond 11+ books. Each paper is **pitched a level above a typical 11+ exam**, providing a greater challenge and stretching skills further. The coverage is matched to the National Curriculum and the National Numeracy Strategy and will also **provide invaluable preparation for higher level Key Stage 2 SATs performance**. One of the key features of Bond Assessment Papers is that each one practises **a wide variety of skills and question types** so that children are always challenged to think – and don't get bored repeating the same question type again and again. We believe that variety is the key to effective learning. It helps children 'think on their feet' and cope with the unexpected.

What does the book contain?

- **24 papers** – each one contains 50 questions.
- **Tutorial links throughout** – [B 5] – this icon appears in the margin next to the questions. It indicates links to the relevant section in *How to do...11+ Maths*, our invaluable subject guide that offers explanations and practice for all core question types.
- **Scoring devices** – there are score boxes in the margins and a Progress Chart on page 72. The chart is a visual and motivating way for children to see how they are doing. It also turns the score into a percentage that can help decide what to do next.
- **Next Step Planner** – advice on what to do after finishing the papers can be found on the inside back cover.
- **Answers** – located in an easily-removed central pull-out section.

How can you use this book?

One of the great strengths of Bond Assessment Papers is their flexibility. They can be used at home, in school and by tutors to:

- set **timed formal practice** tests – allow about 30 minutes per paper in line with standard 11+ demands. Reduce the suggested time limit by five minutes to practise working at speed

- provide **bite-sized chunks** for regular practice
- **highlight strengths and weaknesses** in the core skills
- identify **individual needs**
- set **homework**
- follow **a complete 11+ preparation strategy** alongside *The Parents' Guide to the 11+* (see below).

It is best to start at the beginning and work through the papers in order. Calculators should not be used.

Remind children to check whether each answer needs a unit of measurement before they start a test. If units of measurement are not included in answers that require them, they will lose marks for those questions. To ensure that children can practise including them in their answers, units of measurement have been omitted after the answer rules for some questions.

If you are using the book as part of a careful run-in to the 11+, we suggest that you also have two other essential Bond resources close at hand:

How to do …11+ Maths: the subject guide that explains the question types practised in this book. Use the cross-reference icons to find the relevant sections.

The Parents' Guide to the 11+: the step-by-step guide to the whole 11+ experience. It clearly explains the 11+ process, provides guidance on how to assess children, helps you to set complete action plans for practice and explains how you can use *Maths 11+–12+ Book 1* and *Book 2* as part of a strategic run-in to the exam.

See the inside front cover for more details of these books.

What does a score mean and how can it be improved?

It is unfortunately impossible to guarantee that a child will pass the 11+ exam if they achieve a certain score on any practice book or paper. Success on the day depends on a host of factors, including the scores of the other children sitting the test. However, we can give some guidance on what a score indicates and how to improve it.

If children colour in the Progress Chart on page 72, this will give an idea of present performance in percentage terms. The Next Step Planner inside the back cover will help you to decide what to do next to help a child progress. It is always valuable to go over wrong answers with children. If they are having trouble with any particular question type, follow the tutorial links to *How to do …11+ Maths* for step-by-step explanations and further practice.

Don't forget the website…!

Visit www.bond11plus.co.uk for lots of advice, information and suggestions on everything to do with Bond, the 11+ and helping children to do their best.

Key words

Some special maths words are used in this book. You will find them **in bold** each time they appear in the papers. These words are explained here.

acute angle	an angle that is less than a right angle
coordinates	the two numbers, one horizontal, the other vertical, that plot a point on a grid, e.g. (4, 2)
edge	an edge is where two faces meet on a 3-D shape
factor	the factors of a number are numbers that divide into it, e.g. 1, 2, 4 and 8 are all factors of 8
icosahedron	a solid with 20 plane faces
integer	a positive or negative whole number, e.g. –6, 0, 3
kite	a four-sided shape that looks a stretched diamond
lowest common multiple	The lowest common multiple (LCM) of two numbers is found by first finding the common multiples, then writing down the lowest, e.g. the multiples of 6 are 6, 12, 18, 24, 30, 36, 42, 48, 54, etc. The multiples of 8 are 8, 16, 24, 32, 40, 48, 56, 64, 72, etc. The common multiples of 6 and 8 are 24, 48, 72, etc. So the lowest common multiple is **24**
lowest term	the simplest you can make a fraction, e.g. $\frac{4}{10}$ reduced to the lowest term is $\frac{2}{5}$
mean	a type of average. You find the mean by adding all the scores together and dividing by the number of scores, e.g. the mean of 1, 3 and 8 is 4
median	a type of average. The middle number of a set of numbers after ordering, e.g. the median of 1, 3 and 8 is 3 e.g. the median of 7, 4, 6 and 9 is 6.5 (halfway between 6 and 7)
mixed number	a number that contains a whole number and a fraction, e.g. $5\frac{1}{2}$ is a mixed number
mode	a type of average. The most common number in a set of numbers, e.g. the mode of 2, 3, 2, 7, 2 is 2
obtuse angle	an angle that is more than 90° and not more than 180°
parallelogram	a four-sided shape that has all its opposite sides equal and parallel
polygon	a 2-D shape with straight sides
prime number	any number that can only be divided by itself and 1, e.g. 2, 3 and 7 are prime numbers
range	the difference between the largest and smallest of a set of numbers, e.g. the range of 1, 2, 5, 3, 6, 8 is 7 (8 – 1)
reflex angle	an angle that is bigger than 180° and less than 360°
rhombus	a parallelogram with four equal sides and diagonals crossing at 90°
square root	any number which, when multiplied by itself, gives you the original numhber, e.g. 4 is the square root 16 (4 × 4 = 16; $\sqrt{16} = 4$)
trapezium	a four-sided shape that has only one pair of parallel sides
vertex, vertices	the point where two or more edges or sides in a shape meet

Paper 1

Jill and Jack Brown had a weekend break. They stayed at a different campsite on a Friday and Saturday, returning home on Sunday. They had a similar weekend break a month later. Here are the campsite charges.

Price per night per adult	Campsite
£7.25	Longville
£6.60	Shortown
£12.05	Ingleferry
£8.25	Spocking

1 How much did it cost to camp at Longville and Shortown on the first weekend? _____

2 How much did it cost to camp at Ingleferry and Spocking on the second weekend? _____

3 What was the difference in the camping price of the two weekends? _____

4 How much did the two camping weekends cost them? _____

Work out the values of a, b, c and d in the following.

5 $2a \div 13 = 2$ $a = $ _____

6 $15 + 5b = 50$ $b = $ _____

7 $4c \times 2 = 48$ $c = $ _____

8 $72 - 6d = 6$ $d = $ _____

Now use the values of a, b, c and d above to work out this calculation.

9 $(a + b) \div (d - c) = $ _____

10–12 What numbers come out of the machine?

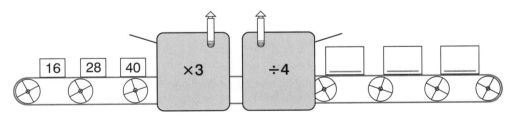

Put >, < or = as appropriate in each of these.

13 6×1.25 ___ $3\frac{1}{2} + 4\frac{1}{4}$

14 3.75×8 ___ $17 + 13$

15 $\frac{10}{26} + \frac{5}{8} + \frac{1}{4}$ ___ $0.75 + 0.8$

16 16% of 225 ___ 6^2

17–19 These are two mirror lines at right angles. Draw the reflected shape of this quadrilateral in sectors A, B and C.

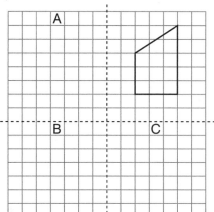

Calculate the answers to these additions.

20 $9^2 + 1^2 = $ ___   **21** $8^2 + 2^2 = $ ___   **22** $7^2 + 3^2 = $ ___

23 $6^2 + 4^2 = $ ___   **24** $5^2 + 5^2 = $ ___

Bill paints model soldiers. For every 2 French soldiers he has 3 English soldiers and 4 Spanish soldiers. If he paints 243 soldiers altogether, how many does he paint of each kind?

25 French soldiers ___   **26** English soldiers ___   **27** Spanish soldiers ___

28–30 Complete this table, turning the fractions into percentages.

Fraction	Percentage
$\frac{4}{40}$	___ %
$\frac{16}{25}$	___ %
$\frac{3}{12}$	___ %

Calculate the answers to these subtractions.

31 $17.93 - 8.2 = $ _____   **32** $496.07 - 219.88 = $ _____

33 $923.17 - 11.76 = $ _____   **34** $334.7 - 208.09 = $ _____

35 $829.87 - 731.98 = $ _____

36–41 16 can be made by multiplying its prime **factors**:
$2 \times 2 \times 2 \times 2$. Write the following as products of prime **factors**.

$12 = $ ___ $\times$ ___ $\times$ ___

$18 = $ ___ $\times$ ___ $\times$ ___

42–45 Complete this table of areas and perimeters of the rectangles.

	Length	Width	Area	Perimeter
Rectangle 1	7 cm	3.5 cm	___ cm²	___ cm
Rectangle 2	11 cm	6.5 cm	___ cm²	___ cm

B 20

4

In a bag of coloured marbles there are 2 red, 4 blue and 6 green marbles.
Circle TRUE or FALSE for each of these statements.

B 16

46 There is a one in six chance of taking out a red marble.   TRUE   FALSE

47 There is a one in four chance of taking out a blue marble.   TRUE   FALSE

48 There is a 50/50 chance of taking out a green marble.   TRUE   FALSE

49 There is a one in twelve chance of taking out a black marble.   TRUE   FALSE

50 If you take 4 of the green marbles out of the bag there will then
be a 50/50 chance of taking out a blue marble.   TRUE   FALSE

5

Now go to the Progress Chart to record your score!   Total   50

Paper 2

1 Vijay the plumber put in a new bathroom for us. He charges £2200 plus $17\frac{1}{2}$% VAT.
What was the total we paid?   _____

B 12

2 A celebration cake has 16 silver stars on it. How many cakes can be
completed using a box of 416 stars?   _____ cakes

B 3

3 Write in figures three million ten thousand three hundred and five.   _____

B 1

4 A school took 75 people on a trip to a local wildlife park. 12% were adults
and 28% were girls. How many boys went?   _____

B 12

4

5–8 Complete this table.

B 11

×	0.6	0.7
0.2	___	___
1.2	___	___

4

Solve these fraction problems.

B 10

9 $\frac{1}{3} + \frac{1}{2} + \frac{1}{6} =$ ___

10 $4 - 1\frac{3}{5} =$ ___

11 $\frac{8}{12} \div \frac{1}{3} =$ ___

12 $\frac{5}{8} \times \frac{3}{7} =$ ___

4

Put the signs $<$, $>$ or $=$ in the correct place. (Remember, calculate what is inside the brackets first.)

13 $(19 - 12) + 6$ ___ $19 - (12 + 6)$ **14** $(15 + 14) - 12$ ___ $15 + (14 - 12)$

15 $(3^2 \times 2^2) + 4$ ___ $3^2 \times (2^2 + 4)$ **16** $18 \div (3 - 2)$ ___ $(18 \div 3) - 2$

17 $6 \times (4 \times 3)$ ___ $(6 \times 4) \times 3$

$2 \times 2 \times 2 = 8$

$2 \times 2 \times 2$ can be written as 2^3 because 2 is multiplied by itself three times. Calculate the answers to these.

18 $3^3 =$ ___   **19** $4^3 =$ ___   **20** $5^3 =$ ___

21–26 Round these numbers.

	To nearest 100	To nearest 1000	To nearest 10 000
54 506			
129 375			

27–29 This line graph shows multiples of 2. Draw lines to represent the multiples of 3, 7 and $\frac{1}{2}$. Label each line.

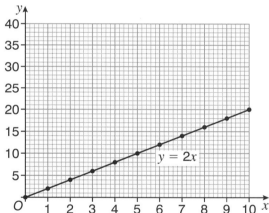

$y = 2x$

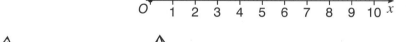

Tetrahedron   Square-based pyramid   Cube

30–35 Complete this table.

	Faces	Vertices	Edges
Tetrahedron	4		
Square-based pyramid		5	
Cube			12

Calculate the number of degrees represented by *a*, *b*, *c* and *d* in these named triangles.

B 18

Isosceles

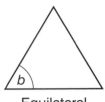

Equilateral

Right-angled

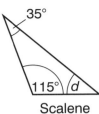

Scalene

36 Angle *a* = ___°

37 Angle *b* = ___°

38 Angle *c* = ___°

39 Angle *d* = ___°

B 6

40 What is the next **prime number** after 13? ___

41 What is the next **prime number** after 23? ___

42–45 What fraction of a turn do you need to make to each of these to fit on their starting positions?

B 10
B 24

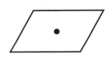

___   ___   ___   ___

Here is a table of charges for small advertisements (ads) in two local newspapers. Use the data to help you answer the questions below. Numbers, amounts of money, and measurements in numbers count as words. So £25 is one word, so is 13 m and 101 is one word too.

B 2
B 3

Price for one week's ad	The Trumpeter	The Flag
Ads up to and including 25 words	£3.60	£3.95
Every word above 25 words (per word)	19p per word	15p per word
Box number	£1.85	£1.55
Headlines above ad	£1.95	£2

Dark pine 3 drawer chest, 3 drawer bedside table and matching single headboard. £60 the lot.
BOX No. 5/103

46 What would this ad cost in The Trumpeter? ___

47 What would be the cost in The Flag? ___

48 What would this ad cost in The Trumpeter? _____

49 What would be the cost in The Flag? _____

50 Would this ad be cheaper in The Trumpeter or The Flag? _____ | 5

Now go to the Progress Chart to record your score! **Total** | 50

Paper 3

1 Write in figures one million two hundred and thirty-five thousand, and three. _____ | B 1

2 A teacher checked his smiley face badges and said, 'I've only got 2.5% of my 280 badge order left.' How many badges were left? _____ | B 12

3 It takes 0.3 m of ribbon to decorate a paper party hat. How many hats can be decorated using 12.3 m of ribbon? _____ | B 11

4 Gerald tiled the floor in our neighbour's kitchen for £860 plus $17\frac{1}{2}$% VAT. What was their total bill? _____ | B 12

| 4

Look at these values for A, B, C and D then work out the answers to the questions below. (Remember, calculate what is inside brackets first.) | B 8

A	B	C	D
570	12	235	30

5 A ÷ D = _____   **6** (A − C) × B = _____   **7** ((B × D) + C) − A = _____ | 3

| B14/B10
| B 12

This pie chart shows how Amelie usually spends her £3 a week pocket money.

8 What fraction of her pocket money goes in her money box? _____

9 What % of her pocket money is spent on swimming? _____

10 What % is spent on comics? _____

11 What fraction goes on sweets? _____

12 What % does she spend on toys? _____ | 5

Swim £1.05 | Sweets 75p | Comics 48p | Toys 42p | Save 30p

Calculate the answers to these fraction problems. Give your answers as fractions or **mixed numbers** in their **lowest terms**.

13 $\frac{1}{2} \times \frac{3}{4}$ = _____

14 $\frac{5}{8} - \frac{1}{24}$ = _____

15 $\frac{5}{6} + \frac{4}{9}$ = _____

16 $3 \div \frac{1}{3}$ = _____

Now calculate the answers to these fraction and percentages problems. Give your answers as fractions or **mixed numbers** in their **lowest terms**.

17 (30% of 35) $- 3\frac{1}{4}$ = _____

18 $12\frac{9}{12} - $ (12% of 50) = _____

19 (65% of 35) $- 21\frac{1}{2}$ = _____

20 $\frac{18}{5} + $ (40% of 15) = _____

Three robots, Archie (A), Brian (B) and Carole (C) are in a maze.

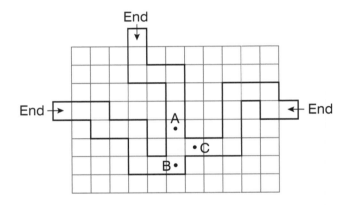

Part of the instructions for each of them to get out is missing. Using F (Forward), R90° (Right 90°) or L90° (Left 90°) write in the missing directions.

21–23 Archie   F3, L90°, _____, _____, _____

24–26 Brian   F2, R90°, F2, _____, F2, _____, _____, L90°, F2

27–29 Carole   F2, L90°, F3, _____, _____, _____, F1, L90°, F1

In a spelling test, ten children got these marks out of thirty.

Esme	Zena	Winston	Simon	Ali	Yasmeen	Frances	Rhiannon	David	Chris
22	27	19	23	9	23	20	16	18	23

30 What is the **range**?   _____

31 What is the **mode**?   _____

32 What is the **median**?   _____

33 What is the **mean**?   _____

34–38 Complete this table.

B 20

Length of the side of a square (cm)	1	2	3	4	5	6	7	8	9	10
Perimeter of square (cm)	4	—	12	—	—	24	—	32	—	40

39 Use the results in the table to help you draw a graph of length against perimeter.

B 14
B 26

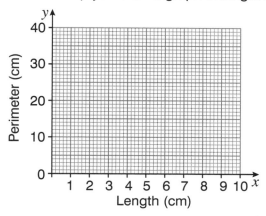

6

40–45 Draw lines to connect the shape with its name.

B 19

        Parallelogram

        Kite

        Octagon

        Hexagon

        Pentagon

        Rhombus

6
B 8

46 $64 - 3p = 37$ $p =$ ___   **47** $4q \times 3 = 84$ $q =$ ___

48 $(5r \div 6) + 8 = 13$ $r =$ ___   **49** $\frac{20s}{25} = 2.4$ $s =$ ___

Now use the values that you have found to work out the value of this.

50 $(3p + 4q) - (2r + 9s) =$ ___

5

Paper 4

Write these in words.

1 $12\frac{3}{5}$ _____

2 $6\frac{7}{8}$ _____

3 $15\frac{12}{19}$ _____

Simplify these expressions.

4 $9a + 7 - 2a + 13 =$ _____

5 $21 - 3b + 5b - 7 =$ _____

6 $3c^2 + 8c^2 - 15 =$ _____

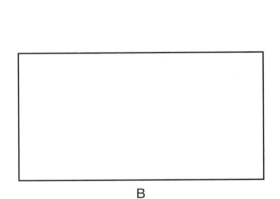

A   B

7–10 Measure the sides of these rectangles to the nearest mm and write the measurements in this table.

	Length (mm)	Width (mm)
Rectangle A	_____	_____
Rectangle B	_____	_____

11–18 Now use your measurements to complete this next table. Convert your measurements to centimetres.

	Length (cm)	Width (cm)	Area (cm²)	Perimeter (cm)
Rectangle A	_____	_____	_____	_____
Rectangle B	_____	_____	_____	_____

In a local shop some items are being sold at a third off. They now cost the following amounts. What was the original, full price?

19 £6.46 _____   20 £58.24 _____   21 £114.28 _____

22 £12.50 _____   23 £10.86 _____

I recently had some goods delivered in these open top boxes. I then unfolded both boxes and laid them out flat.

A

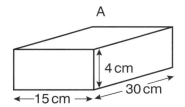

B

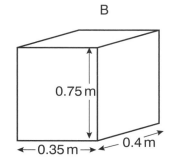

24 What was the surface area of box A when laid flat?   _____ cm²

25 What was the surface area of box B when laid flat?   _____ m²

Bill has been going through his gardening catalogue to order some items for next year. Here are the prices of some of the things he looked at.

Varieties	Potatoes/ bag	Varieties	Onions/ bag	Varieties	Shallots/ bag
Swift	£5.95	Setton	£2.65	Golden Gourmet	£2.65
Lady Balfour	£6.25	Sturon	£2.60	Pikant	£2.95
King Edward	£5.75	Red Baron	£2.75	Jermor	£3.70

26 Bill bought 2 bags of Swift, 2 of Lady Balfour and 1 of King Edward.
How much did he spend on potatoes?   _____

27 He decided to have 2 bags of each of the onions.
How much did that come to?   _____

28 For shallots he decided to have 2 bags of Golden Gourmet and 1 each
of Pikant and Jermor. How much did he spend on these?   _____

29 How much did Bill spend altogether?   _____

30 Bill loaned his catalogue to Seth who decided to buy 2 bags of King Edward
potatoes, 1 bag of Sturon onions and 1 bag of Golden Gourmet shallots.
How much did Seth spend?   _____

A local smallholder is putting animals in different fields. She puts them in different ratios. B 13

31–32 She split the 78 cows in the ratio 5 : 8.
How many are in each field?   ___ : ___.

33–35 She split the 54 pigs in the ratio 1 : 2 : 3.
How many are in each field?   ___ : ___ : ___

36–38 She split the 154 chickens in the ratio 2 : 3 : 6.
How many are in each field?   ___ : ___ : ___   **8**

B 13

39–40 The **factors** of 15 are: 1, ___, ___ and 15

41–45 The **factors** of 24 are: 1, 2, ___, ___, ___, ___, ___ and 24   **7**

B 5

46 What is the **mean** of this set of children's heights?

132 cm   135 cm   138 cm   138 cm   141 cm   142 cm   133 cm   _____ cm

47 What is the **mean** of this set of adults' heights?

1.75 m   1.68 m   1.72 m   1.8 m   1.85 m   _____ m   **2**

48–50 Complete this table.

B 1
B 3

	× 10	× 100	× 1000
0.175	1.75	_____	175
1.004	_____	100.4	_____

Now go to the Progress Chart to record your score!   Total   **50**

Paper 5

Write these in figures.   B 1

   1 Three and a half thousand   _____

   2 Five point six million   _____

   3 Nine hundred and three thousand and ninety-three   _____

   4 Ten point seven million   _____   **4**

Calculate the answers to these subtraction problems.   B 2

   5 5937 − 1989 = _____   **6** 3201 − 2873 = _____

   7 4343 − 2654 = _____   **8** 8017 − 6128 = _____   **4**

This is a graph of square numbers. It can be used to find approximate square numbers and **square roots**. For example, look at the number 5, go up to the curve and across and you will find that the square of 5 is 25.

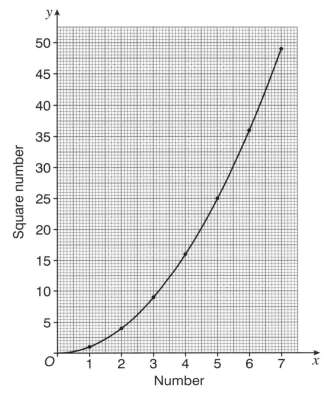

Use the graph to help answer these. Circle the approximate answer.

9 The **square root** of 30 is about: 5.00   5.25   5.5   5.75   6.00

10 The **square root** of 12 is about: 3.25   3.5   3.75   4.00   4.25

11 The **square root** of 21 is about: 4.3   4.4   4.5   4.6   4.7

12 The **square root** of 40 is about: 6.3   6.4   6.5   6.6   6.7

Now find the approximate answers here. Circle the appropriate answer.

13 2.5 squared is about: 6.00   6.25   6.5   6.75   7.00

14 6.5 squared is about: 41.0   41.5   42.0   42.5   43.0

15 1.6 squared is about: 1.5   2.0   2.5   3.0   3.5

16 5.8 squared is about: 32   32.5   33   33.5   34

17–22 Put these masses in the correct order from lightest to heaviest.

500 g $\frac{3}{4}$ kg   0.25 kg   1300 g   800 g $1\frac{1}{3}$ kg

____   ____   ____   ____   ____   ____

A local pig breeder has these fields. Calculate the area and the perimeter of each one.

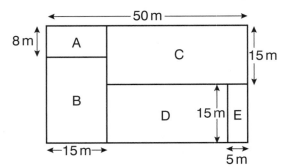

23–24 Field A has a perimeter of _____ m and an area of _____ m².

25–26 Field B has a perimeter of _____ m and an area of _____ m².

27–28 Field C has a perimeter of _____ m and an area of _____ m².

29–30 Field D has a perimeter of _____ m and an area of _____ m².

31–32 Field E has a perimeter of _____ m and an area of _____ m².

Find the values that *a*, *b*, *c* and *d* represent.

33 $4a \div 3 = 8$ $a = \underline{}$

34 $6b - 5 = 7$ $b = \underline{}$

35 $2c - 6 = c + 2$ $c = \underline{}$

36 $2d = 3c$ $d = \underline{}$

Name the shapes that make up this arrow.

37 Shape *a* is a   _____

38 Shape *b* is an   _____

39 Shape *c* is a   _____

40 Shape *d* is a   _____

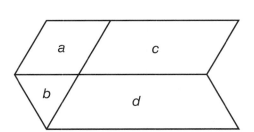

What will these digital clocks read in 38 minutes time?

A. `09:47`   B. `11:50`   C. `15:28`

41 A __ : __   **42** B __ : __   **43** C __ : __

Put the missing number in this sequence.

44 11.04 _____ 11.94 12.39

Write the **coordinates** for this shape.

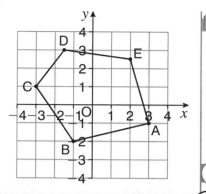

45 A (—, —)   **46** B (—, —)

47 C (—, —)   **48** D (—, —)

49 E (—, —)

50 What is the full name of the shape?

_____

Now go to the Progress Chart to record your score!   **Total**

6

50

Paper 6

Solve these calculations.

1 4.02 − 3.05 =   _____

2 23.43 − 5.1 =   _____

3 67 kg − 500 g =   _____ kg

4 4.7 km − 500 m = _____ km

5 32.7 cm − 3.2 mm = _____ cm

B11/B25

5

Solve these money problems.

6 £43.05 − £1.59 = _____

7 503p + £27.99 = _____

8 £19 ÷ 4 =   _____

9 £4.32 × 9 =   _____

B1/B2

B 3

4

Measure the lengths and widths of these rectangles to the nearest millimetre.

B 26

A

10–11 A: Length _____ mm

Width _____ mm

12–13 B: Length _____ mm

Width _____ mm

B

Now calculate the area and perimeter of each rectangle, giving your answers in either cm² or cm.

14–15 A: Area _____   Perimeter _____

16–17 B: Area _____   Perimeter _____

Work out the value of x in this expression.

18 $3x \div 2 = 9$ $x =$ ___

Circle two of these that give the same value for x as above.

19–20 $2x - 6 = 12$ $2x \times 4 = 48$ $50 - 5x = 9$ $34 - 3x = 16$

Work out the answers to these fraction problems. Give your answers as **mixed numbers** in the **lowest terms**.

21 $32 \div 7 =$ ___   **22** $44 \div 8 =$ ___   **23** $\frac{1}{7} \times 17 =$ ___

24 $\frac{1}{6} \times 27 =$ ___   **25** $\frac{1}{3} + \frac{5}{6} + \frac{4}{9} =$ ___

Calculate the angles x, y and z in these triangles.

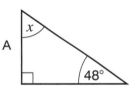 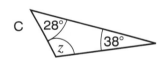

26 A: $x =$ _____   **27** B: $y =$ _____   **28** C: $z =$ _____

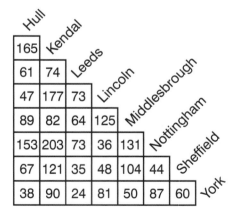

This mileage chart gives distances in miles between places.

29 How far is it to go from Kendal to Middlesbrough and then Middlesbrough to York?   _____ miles

30 How far is it from Nottingham to Leeds and then Leeds to Hull   _____ miles

31 How far is it from York to Lincoln and then Lincoln to Leeds?   _____ miles

5 miles is equivalent to 8 kilometres. Use this fact and the mileage chart to answer these.

32 How many kilometres is it from Kendal to York? _____ km

33 How many kilometres is it from Sheffield to York? _____ km

34 How many kilometres is it from Lincoln to Middlesbrough? _____ km

Put the appropriate sign $<$, $>$ or $=$ in the following. Remember, calculate what is inside brackets first.

35 7^2 ___ $2 \times 3 \times 8$ **36** $(7 \times 20) + 4$ ___ 12^2 **37** $96 \div 4$ ___ 5^2

38 17×10 ___ 13^2 **39** 8^2 ___ $(5 \times 12) + 4$

40–43 Complete this timetable for Bus 2 using the times of travel for Bus 1.

	Bus 1	Bus 2
Swindon	12:10	13:50
Wootton Bassett	12:33	_____
Lyneham	12:40	_____
Calne	12:55	_____
Chippenham	13:07	_____

Put the missing numbers in these sequences.

44 $\frac{1}{6}$ $\frac{1}{3}$ $\frac{1}{2}$ _____ $\frac{5}{6}$

45 $\frac{3}{8}$ $\frac{7}{8}$ $1\frac{3}{8}$ _____ $2\frac{3}{8}$

46 $\frac{5}{12}$ $1\frac{11}{12}$ $3\frac{5}{12}$ _____

The bar chart shows the heights of a class of children.

47 What is the **range** of heights?

_____

48 How many children are taller than 150 cm? _____

49 How many children are shorter than 144 cm? _____

50 What is the **median** height? _____

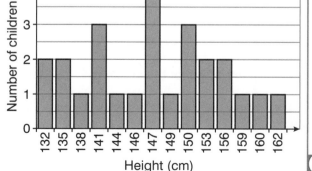

Height (cm)

Now go to the Progress Chart to record your score!   Total   50

17

Paper 7

Remember to work out brackets first, then ÷ and ×, then + and −. Find the answers to the following.

1 $(6 − 5) + 4 =$ _____

2 $6 − (5 + 4) =$ _____

3 $(3 × 2) + 1 =$ _____

4 $3 × (2 + 1) =$ _____

Put brackets in these to produce the given answers.

5 $5 − 4 + 2 = 3$

6 $5 − 4 + 2 = −1$

A new office block has four floors above ground and four below. The lift buttons are shown here.

7 If I enter the lift on floor −3, go up five floors then down two which floor do I exit at? _____

8 If I enter the lift on floor 4, go down seven floors then up two which floor do I exit at? _____

9 If I enter the lift on the ground floor, go down three floors then up six which floor do I exit at? _____

Floor 4 **4**

Floor 3 **3**

Floor 2 **2**

Floor 1 **1**

Floor 0 **0**   Ground Floor

Floor −1 **−1**

Floor −2 **−2**

Floor −3 **−3**

Floor −4 **−4**

What are the **square roots** of these numbers?

10 36 _____

11 169 _____

12 121 _____

13 400 _____

14 225 _____

Look at these shapes.

 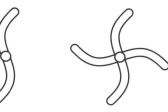 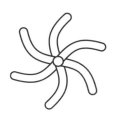

What fraction of a turn should you make before each shape fits exactly on its starting position?

15 A _____   **16** B _____   **17** C _____   **18** D _____

Use a protractor to find the angles in these triangles to the nearest 1°.

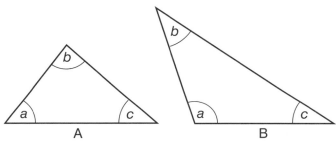

19–21 Triangle A: angle a _____°, angle b _____°, angle c _____°

22–24 Triangle B: angle a _____°, angle b _____°, angle c _____°

You have two normal dice.

25 If you roll one dice what is the chance that you will roll an even number? _____

26 If you roll one dice and roll a 1 what is the chance of rolling a 1 with the other dice? _____

27 If you roll both dice what is the most likely total you will get? _____

Simplify these expressions.

28 $5x + 4x - x + y =$ _____

29 $2y + 5y - 3y + 2z =$ _____

30 $4a + 5a - 2a + 6b - 2b + 3b =$ _____

31 The perimeter of a square is 28 cm. What is its area? _____

32–33 What are the area and perimeter of a square that has sides twice as long as the square in the previous question? Area is _____ and perimeter is _____ .

If $y = 2x + 2$ what is the value of x when:

34 y is 6? $\qquad x = \underline{\hphantom{xx}}$

35 y is 9? $\qquad x = \underline{\hphantom{xx}}$

Find the following missing numbers.

36 $7.5 \times \underline{\hphantom{xx}} = 45$

37 $12.5 \times \underline{\hphantom{xx}} = 87.5$

38 $86 \div \underline{\hphantom{xx}} = 21.5$

39 $24.6 \div \underline{\hphantom{xx}} = 8.2$

Write these fractions as percentages.

40 $\frac{3}{5}$ $\qquad\qquad$ __%

41 $\frac{1}{8}$ $\qquad\qquad$ __%

42 $\frac{11}{20}$ $\qquad\qquad$ __%

Jed Thumper, who bats at number eight, had an average (**mean**) of 14 last year. So far this year he has had these scores.

$\quad$ 20 $\quad$ 0 $\quad$ 14 $\quad$ 19 $\quad$ 26 $\quad$ 12 $\quad$ 14 $\quad$ 23 $\quad$ 7

43 What is Jed's average this season so far? $\qquad$ _____

44 What are the total runs Jed would need to get in his next three innings to get his average up to 16? $\qquad$ _____

Calculate the size of the angles marked with a letter.

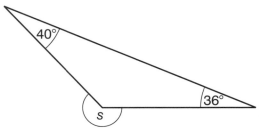

45 What is the size of angle s? $\qquad$ _____

46 What is the size of angle t? $\qquad$ _____

The products of the 5 times table always end with a 5 or a 0. It can be drawn as digits linked by arrows like this.

Here are some further digits, linked by arrows. Can you work out which times table each represents?

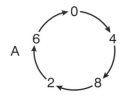

A
B
C
D

47 A is the _____ times table.

48 B is the _____ times table.

49 C is the _____ times table.

50 D is the _____ times table.

4

Now go to the Progress Chart to record your score!   Total   50

Paper 8

Calculate the answers to these multiplications.

1 15 × 17 = _____

2 14 × 12 = _____

3 19 × 19 = _____

B 3

3

Circle the best approximation for the answers to these.

B 3

4 89 × 71 =	6100	6200	6300	6400	6500
5 102 × 267 =	26 000	27 000	28 000	29 000	30 000
6 412 × 497 =	170 000	180 000	190 000	200 000	210 000

3

7–10 Link each fraction calculation with its whole number answer.

B 10

$$\frac{87}{27} + \frac{7}{9} \qquad \mathbf{3}$$

$$\frac{2}{3} + \frac{8}{24} \qquad \mathbf{2}$$

$$\frac{9}{7} + \frac{10}{14} \qquad \mathbf{4}$$

$$\frac{21}{8} + \frac{3}{8} \qquad \mathbf{1}$$

4

21

Underline the correct answer.

11 minutes in $1\frac{1}{4}$ hours	65	70	75	80	85	
12 cm in a km	100 000	101 000	102 000	103 000	104 000	
13 degrees in a semi-circle	360°	90°	45°	180°	270°	
14 seconds in $\frac{3}{4}$ hour	2600	2700	2800	2900	3000	
15 total days in March, April and May	89	90	91	92	93	

5

Use a ruler to measure the sides of this triangle to the nearest millimetre.

B 26

B 20

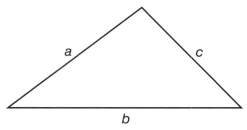

16 $a =$ _____ **17** $b =$ _____ **18** $c =$ _____

19 What is the perimeter of the triangle in centimetres? _____

4

20–23 Complete this table putting in the values of y when $y = \frac{3}{4}x$.

x	1	2	3	4
y	____	____	____	____

B8/B10

4

Find the values.

B8/B6

24 $2x + y = 8$; $\quad y = 6^2 - (2 \times 17)$: $\qquad x =$ _____

25 $\frac{2}{3}r - s = 1$; $\quad s = (6 \times 4) \div 8$: $\qquad r =$ _____

26 $3a + 2c = 36$; $\quad c = 3^3 - 21$: $\qquad a =$ _____

3

Name the lettered shapes in this drawing of a boat.

B 19

27 a _____

28 b _____

29 c _____

30 d _____

31 e _____

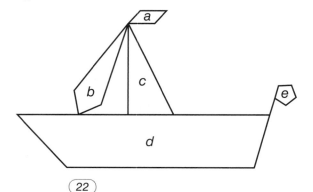

5

Our small local cinema has four screens. Last week the number of people viewing each film were displayed in this pie chart. The total number of people who went to the cinema was 1440.

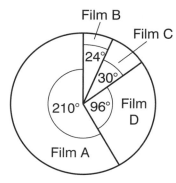

Film B
Film C
24°
30°
210° 96° Film D
Film A

B14/B10
B 2

32 How many people saw the most popular film? _____

33 What fraction of people, in **lowest terms**, went to see Film B? _____

34 How many more people saw Film D than Film B? _____

35 How many people watched Film C? _____   4

Work out the values that f, g and h represent in these equations.

B8/B6

36 $f^2 + 3f = 18$ $f =$ _____

37 $5g + g^2 = 50$ $g =$ _____

38 $2h + 3h + 4h^2 = 84$ $h =$ _____   3

Calculate the areas of these triangles. Scale: each square is 1 cm by 1 cm.

B 18

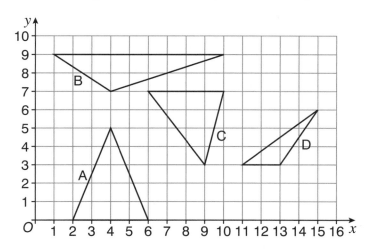

39 Triangle A has an area of _____

40 Triangle B has an area of _____

41 Triangle C has an area of _____

42 Triangle D has an area of _____   4

Mr and Mrs Awn run a caravan and camping site. It is open from March to October. The table shows the percentage of visitors in each of these months last year. In total they had 600 visitors.

B 12
B 2

March	2%
April	5%
May	9%
June	8%
July	20%
August	24%
September	22%
October	10%

43 How many visitors were there in August? _____

44 How many visitors were there in May? _____

45 How many more visitors were there in September than in April? _____

46 How many fewer visitors stayed in March than in July? _____

○ 4

A nearby attraction is the River Festival.

47 Over the summer 3026 tickets were sold. Each ticket costs £3.25.
What amount of money was taken? £ _____

B 3

48 People entered the raft race and paid £1.45 each to enter. The total sum taken was £397.30. How many entries were there? _____

B 3

49 The organisers give winners' rosettes for each of the 48 main races.
The rosettes cost 98p each. How much was spent on rosettes? £ _____

B 3

50 Overall, the River Festival made £12 858.56. The organisers spent £6429.28 running the festival. How much was the profit, as a percentage of the total money made? _____%

B2/B12
○ 4

Now go to the Progress Chart to record your score!   Total ○ 50

Paper 9

Write in the answers to these calculations.

B 2

1 1579 + 3241 = _____

2 1978 + 5539 = _____

3 2736 + 7889 = _____

4 3862 + 5358 = _____

○ 4

Find the answers to these fraction calculations, giving your answers in their **lowest terms**.

5 $5\frac{2}{3} + 3\frac{11}{12} =$ _____

6 $6\frac{1}{2} + 4\frac{5}{8} =$ _____

7 $4\frac{3}{7} + 2\frac{18}{21} =$ _____

8 $9\frac{9}{20} + 2\frac{3}{5} =$ _____

Here is part of a bus timetable.

	BUS A ↓	BUS B ↑
Cheltenham	12:10	18:00
Seven Springs	12:15	17:39
Colesbourne	12:30	17:34
North Cerney	12:35	17:29
Cirencester	12:58	17:05
Siddington	13:03	17:02
South Cerney	13:12	16:53
Latton	13:19	16:46
Cricklade	13:25	16:41
Blunsdon	13:33	16:33
Swindon	13:50	16:20

9 How long do these two buses take in each direction? _____ h _____ min

10 What is the shortest time between stops for either bus? _____ minutes

11 What is the longest time between stops for either bus? _____ minutes

12 How long does it take to travel from Cricklade to Colesbourne? _____ minutes

13 One day Bus A is delayed at North Cerney for four minutes and then for twelve minutes at Latton. What time did it arrive in Swindon? ___ : ___

Calculate the answers to these decimal problems.

14 $19.3 \times 2.3 =$ _____

15 $8.6 \times 5.6 =$ _____

16 $13.76 \div 8 =$ _____

17 $102.2 \div 7 =$ _____

These are the average scores of the players in my local cricket team for last season.

21   22   26   20   17   19   19   14   12   9   8

18 What was last year's team **mean**? _____

19 What was last year's **mode**? _____

20 What was last year's **range**? _____

4.23376

21 What is this number to two decimal places? _____

22 What is this number to three decimal places? _____

23–25 Reflect these shapes in the mirror line.

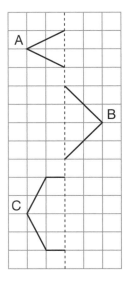

What are the names of the shapes that you have made?

26 Shape A _____   **27** Shape B _____   **28** Shape C _____

Use these equivalents to answer the questions below.

Imperial	Metric
1 gallon	4.5 litres (l)
2.2 pounds (lb)	1 kilogram (kg)
5 miles	8 kilometres (km)
1 ounce (oz)	30 grams (g)

Imperial
16 ounces (oz) = 1 pound (lb)
1760 yards (yd) = 1 mile

29 3 gallons ≈ _____ litres

30 44 lb ≈ _____ kg

31 0.3 kg ≈ _____ oz

32 1 km ≈ _____ yards

33 $4\frac{1}{2}$ oz ≈ _____ g

12 can be made from its prime **factors**, 2 and 3: 12 = 2 × 2 × 3. What are the prime **factors** to make the numbers below?

34–35 21   Prime **factors** ___ and ___

36–37 28   Prime **factors** ___ and ___

38 27   Prime **factor** ___

Work out the values that p, q and r represent in these.

39 $15 - 2p = 9$ $p = $ ___

40 $3q - 4^2 = 5$ $q = $ ___

41 $6r - 5^2 = 5$ $r = $ ___

Use the values of p, q and r above to solve this equation.

42 $4p + 2q - 3r = $ ___

Find the missing numbers in these.

43 $16.8 - $ ___ $= 3.75$

44 ___ $+ 2.34 = 16.08$

45 $3.5 + $ ___ $- 4.9 = 12.85$

46 ___ $+ 9.6 - 1.35 = 17.95$

Calculate the areas of these triangles. Scale: each small square is 2 mm × 2 mm.

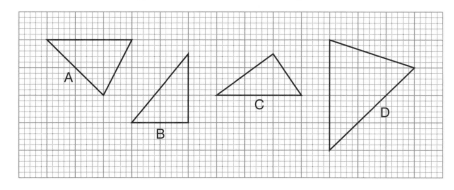

47 Area of triangle A =   _____ cm²

48 Area of triangle B =   _____ cm²

49 Area of triangle C =   _____ cm²

50 Area of triangle D =   _____ cm²

Now go to the Progress Chart to record your score!   Total   50

Paper 10

1 What is the chance of spinning a red? _____

2 What is the chance of spinning a purple, blue or green? _____

3 What is the chance of spinning an orange or yellow? _____

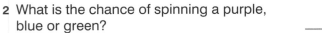

Spinner A

4 What is the chance of spinning a 3? _____

5 What is the chance of spinning a 2? _____

6 What is the chance of spinning a 1? _____

Spinner B

	Arkville	Bellton	Cracklewood
Midday	5 °C	7 °C	3 °C
Midnight	−6 °C	−2 °C	−9 °C

These are the temperatures in three villages yesterday.

7 What is the difference in temperature in Arkville between midday and midnight? _____°C

8 What is the difference between the temperature in Bellton at midday and the temperature in Cracklewood at midnight? _____°C

9 What is the difference between the temperature in Arkville at midnight and the temperature in Cracklewood at midday? _____°C

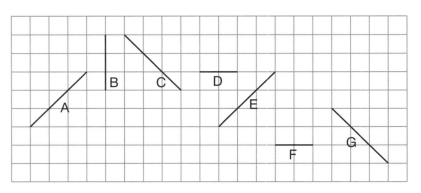

Use these terms to fill in the blanks: parallel, vertical, horizontal, perpendicular.

10 B is a _____ line

11 F is _____ to D

12 A is _____ to G

13 D is a _____ line

Calculate the answers to these money problems.

14 What is the total of £205.32, £4.69 and £15.06? _____ B 2

15 2050 people visit an attraction paying £4.50 per ticket.
How much was taken altogether? _____ B 3

16 What would be the price of goods costing £11.88 if they were
offered at $\frac{1}{3}$ off? _____ B 10

17 What is the cost of 8 articles at £1.65 each? _____ B 3

4

Xiang, Kira and Rebecca work at the local garden centre. This table shows how many
hours each works in a week, and how much pay they receive. Use the information to
calculate how much each person earns per hour. B 3

	Xiang	**Kira**	**Rebecca**
Pay	£227.50	£300	£250
Hours worked	35 hours	40 hours	40 hours

18 What does Xiang get per hour? _____

19 What does Kira get per hour? _____

20 What does Rebecca get per hour? _____

3

Look at these squares. What numbers do A, B and C represent? B 7

4.5	6	7.5
3	4.5	6
A	3	4.5

101	110	B
92	101	110
83	92	101

3.15	4.35	5.55
1.95	3.15	4.35
C	1.95	3.15

21 A is _____

22 B is _____

23 C is _____

3

Write these in figures. B 1

24 One hundred and seven point three five _____

25 Thirty-one and eleven sixteenths _____

26 Zero point one five seven five _____

3

(29)

Find the values in these expressions.

27 $x^2 + y = 32;$ $\qquad y = 105 - 98$ $\qquad\qquad\qquad x = $ _____

28 $4az + 15 = 39;$ $\qquad z = 7^2 - (5^2 + 21)$ $\qquad\qquad a = $ _____

29 $13p + 5q = 82;$ $\qquad q = 3^2 - 3$ $\qquad\qquad\qquad p = $ _____

30–32 Reflect these shapes in the mirror line.

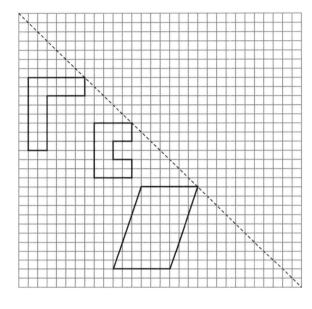

Calculate the answers to these.

33 $9^2 - 1^2 = $ $\qquad\qquad\qquad\qquad\qquad\qquad$ _____

34 $8^2 - 2^2 = $ $\qquad\qquad\qquad\qquad\qquad\qquad$ _____

35 $7^2 - 3^2 = $ $\qquad\qquad\qquad\qquad\qquad\qquad$ _____

36 $6^2 - 4^2 = $ $\qquad\qquad\qquad\qquad\qquad\qquad$ _____

37 $5^2 - 5^2 = $ $\qquad\qquad\qquad\qquad\qquad\qquad$ _____

Work out the least number of cubes needed to fill out each shape so that it is a solid cuboid.

A

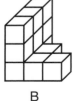

B

C

38 A _____ cubes $\qquad$ **39** B _____ cubes $\qquad$ **40** C _____ cubes

Calculate these fractions and percentages.

41 $\frac{2}{3}$ of 270 = _____

42 $\frac{4}{5}$ of 575 = _____

43 12% of 800 = _____

44 $\frac{3}{8}$ of 104 = _____

45 5% of 0.5 = _____

5

46–50 Calculate the angles marked with a letter.

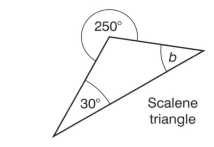

Scalene triangle

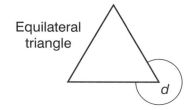

Equilateral triangle

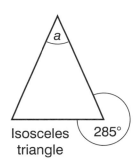

Isosceles triangle

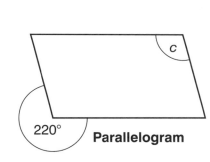

Parallelogram

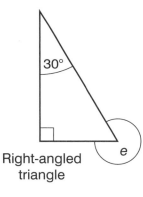

Right-angled triangle

a = _____   *b* = _____   *c* = _____   *d* = _____   *e* = _____

5

Now go to the Progress Chart to record your score!   Total   **50**

Paper 11

1–4 List all of the **prime numbers** between 10 and 20.

_____   _____   _____   _____

4

5–8 Circle all of the numbers here that are exactly divisible by 8.

708   816   1028   2096   198   324   176   424

4

9–13 Plot the points $(-2, 1)$, $(-5, 1)$, $(-2, 5)$, $(-5, 5)$ on the grid and then draw the rectangle that they define.

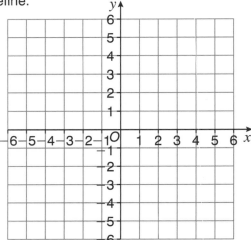

14 Now translate the rectangle 7 units to the right and 3 units down and draw the rectangle there.

15–17 Use a protractor to measure the angles in this triangle to the nearest 1°.

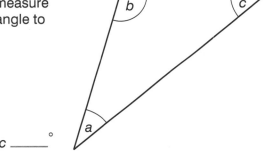

a _____°, b _____°, c _____°

Ms Bright brought an egg-timer to school the other day. Here are the estimates that some of the children in her class made as to how long it would take for the sand to run through the egg-timer glass. The actual time was 3 minutes 46 seconds.

Aileen	230 seconds
Alejandra	4 minutes
Chris	200 seconds
Davina	3 minutes 40 seconds
Edward	$4\frac{1}{4}$ minutes

18 Whose was the nearest estimate? _____

19 Whose estimate was furthest away? _____

20 What was the time difference between these two? _____

21 What was the difference between Alejandra's and Chris' estimate? _____

22 What was the **range** of the estimates? _____

Mr and Mrs Lin decided to take up painting and attend an art workshop. The workshop was £35 per person. They needed to buy some art materials and the table here shows the prices of the things that they chose.

Watercolour paint set	£16.13
Acrylic paint set	£11.99
Watercolour brush set	£12.55
Acrylic brush set	£8.65
Watercolour paper	£12.51
Acrylic paper	£6.30

23 Mrs Lin wanted to use acrylics. How much did it cost her for acrylic paints, brushes and paper altogether? _____

24 Mr Lin wanted to use watercolours. How much did it cost him for watercolour paints, brushes and paper altogether? _____

25 How much did they pay altogether, including the price of the workshop? _____

26 How much more than Mrs Lin did Mr Lin pay for his materials? _____

4

Make 60 from its prime **factors**.

27–30 60 = _____ × _____ × _____ × _____

4

31–33 Work out the input numbers to this function machine.

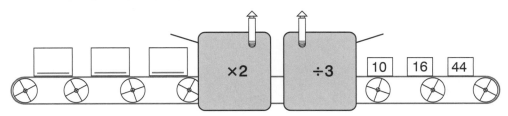

3

Change the fractions into percentages, and percentages into fractions in their **lowest terms**.

34 30% _____

35 $\frac{12}{15}$ _____%

36 $\frac{13}{20}$ _____%

37 80% _____

4

33

38–43 Complete this table of multiplications.

×		0.5	0.8
	1.2	3.0	4.8
0.1		0.05	
	0.04		0.16

6

How many lines of symmetry are there in these shapes?

44 An equilateral triangle _____

45 A square _____

46 A regular pentagon _____

Bill grew some sunflowers this year. He measured the six tallest. Here are the heights.

1.63 m   1.58 m   1.71 m   1.63 m   1.57 m   1.60 m

47 What is the **mode**? _____

48 What is the **mean**? _____

49 What is the **median**? _____

50 What is the **range** in centimetres? _____

Now go to the Progress Chart to record your score! **Total** 50

Paper 12

1–6 Round each of these numbers to two decimal places and to one decimal place.

	Two decimal places	One decimal place
4.1454	_____	_____
3.066	_____	_____
10.816	_____	_____

Any answer that requires units of measurement should be marked wrong if the correct units have not been included.

Paper 1

1 £27.70
2 £40.60
3 £12.90
4 £68.30
5 13
6 7
7 6
8 11
9 4
10 12
11 21
12 30
13 <
14 =
15 <
16 =
17–19

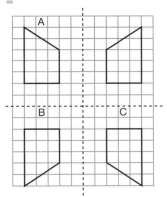

20 82
21 68
22 58
23 52
24 50
25 54
26 81
27 108
28 10
29 64
30 25
31 9.73
32 276.19
33 911.41
34 126.61
35 97.89
36–38 2, 2, 3
39–41 2, 3, 3
42 24.5
43 21
44 71.5
45 35
46 TRUE
47 FALSE
48 TRUE
49 FALSE
50 TRUE

Paper 2

1 £2585
2 26
3 3 010 305
4 45
5–8

×	0.6	0.7
0.2	**0.12**	**0.14**
1.2	**0.72**	**0.84**

9 1
10 $2\frac{2}{5}$
11 2
12 $\frac{15}{56}$
13 >
14 =
15 <
16 >
17 =
18 27
19 64
20 125
21–26

	To nearest 100	To nearest 1000	To nearest 10 000
54 506	**54 500**	**55 000**	**50 000**
129 375	**129 400**	**129 000**	**130 000**

27–29

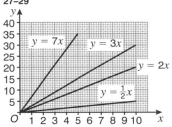

30–35

	Faces	Vertices	Edges
Tetrahedron	4	**4**	**6**
Square-based pyramid	**5**	5	**8**
Cube	**6**	**8**	12

36 66
37 60
38 40
39 30
40 17
41 29
42 $\frac{1}{3}$
43 $\frac{1}{2}$
44 $\frac{1}{5}$
45 $\frac{1}{2}$
46 £5.45
47 £5.50
48 £6.02
49 £5.95
50 The Trumpeter

Paper 3

1 1 235 003
2 7
3 41
4 £1010.50
5 19
6 4020
7 25
8 $\frac{1}{10}$
9 35%
10 16%
11 $\frac{1}{4}$
12 14%
13 $\frac{3}{8}$
14 $\frac{7}{12}$
15 $1\frac{5}{18}$
16 9
17 $7\frac{1}{4}$
18 $6\frac{3}{4}$
19 $1\frac{1}{4}$
20 $9\frac{3}{5}$
21 F2
22 R90°
23 F2
24 L90°
25 R90°
26 F1
27 R90°
28 F2
29 R90°
30 18
31 23
32 21
33 20
34–38

Length of the side of a square (cm)	1	2	3	4	5	6	7	8	9	10
Perimeter of square (cm)	4	**8**	12	**16**	**20**	24	**28**	32	**36**	40

39

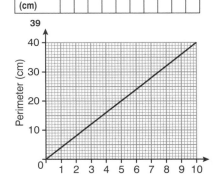

40–45

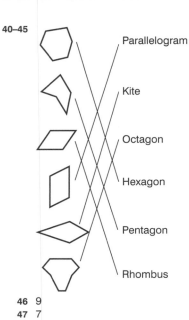

- Parallelogram
- Kite
- Octagon
- Hexagon
- Pentagon
- Rhombus

46 9
47 7
48 6
49 3
50 16

Paper 4

1 twelve and three fifths
2 six and seven eighths
3 fifteen and twelve nineteenths
4 $7a + 20$
5 $2b + 14$ or $2(b + 7)$
6 $11c^2 - 15$

7–10

	Length (mm)	Width (mm)
Rectangle A	70	55
Rectangle B	65	35

11–18

	Length (cm)	Width (cm)	Area (cm²)	Perimeter (cm)
Rectangle A	7	5.5	38.5	25
Rectangle B	6.5	3.5	22.75	20

19 £9.69
20 £87.36
21 £171.42
22 £18.75
23 £16.29
24 810
25 1.265
26 £30.15
27 £16.00
28 £11.95
29 £58.10
30 £16.75

31–32 30 : 48
33–35 9 : 18 : 27
36–38 28 : 42 : 84
39–40 3, 5
41–45 3, 4, 6, 8, 12
46 137
47 1.76

48–50

	×10	×100	×1000
0.175	1.75	**17.5**	175
1.004	**10.04**	100.4	**1004**

Paper 5

1 3500
2 5 600 000
3 903 093
4 10 700 000
5 3948
6 328
7 1689
8 1889
9 5.5
10 3.5
11 4.6
12 6.3
13 6.25
14 42.5
15 2.5
16 33.5
17 0.25 kg
18 500 g
19 $\frac{3}{4}$ kg
20 800 g
21 1300 g
22 $1\frac{1}{3}$ kg
23 46
24 120
25 74
26 330
27 100
28 525
29 90
30 450
31 40
32 75
33 6
34 2
35 8
36 12
37 rhombus
38 equilateral triangle
39 parallelogram
40 trapezium
41 10:25
42 12:28
43 16:06
44 11.49
45 $(3, -1)$

46 $(-1, -2)$
47 $(-3, 1)$
48 $(-1.5, 3)$
49 $(2, 2.5)$
50 Irregular pentagon

Paper 6

1 0.97
2 18.33
3 66.5
4 4.2
5 32.38
6 £41.46
7 £33.02
8 £4.75
9 £38.88
10 135
11 35
12 96
13 25
14 47.25 cm²
15 34 cm
16 24 cm²
17 24.2 cm
18 6
19 $2x \times 4 = 48$
20 $34 - 3x = 16$
21 $4\frac{4}{7}$
22 $5\frac{1}{2}$
23 $2\frac{3}{7}$
24 $4\frac{1}{2}$
25 $1\frac{11}{18}$
26 42°
27 74°
28 114°
29 132
30 134
31 154
32 144
33 96
34 200
35 $>$
36 $=$
37 $<$
38 $>$
39 $=$
40 14:13
41 14:20
42 14:35
43 14:47
44 $\frac{2}{3}$
45 $1\frac{7}{8}$
46 $4\frac{11}{12}$
47 30 cm
48 7
49 8
50 147 cm

Paper 7

1. 5
2. −3
3. 7
4. 9
5. $(5 − 4) + 2 = 3$
6. $5 − (4 + 2) = −1$
7. Floor 0 − Ground floor
8. Floor −1
9. Floor 3
10. 6
11. 13
12. 11
13. 20
14. 15
15. $\frac{1}{3}$
16. $\frac{1}{2}$
17. $\frac{1}{4}$
18. $\frac{1}{6}$

19–21. 53, 85, 42
22–24. 108, 38, 34

25. $\frac{1}{2}$
26. $\frac{1}{6}$
27. 7
28. $8x + y$
29. $4y + 2z$
30. $7a + 7b$ or $7(a + b)$
31. 49 cm²
32. 196 cm²
33. 56 cm
34. 2
35. 3.5 or $3\frac{1}{2}$
36. 6
37. 7
38. 4
39. 3
40. 60
41. 12.5 or $12\frac{1}{2}$
42. 55
43. 15
44. 57
45. 256°
46. 242°
47. 4
48. 8
49. 2
50. 6

Paper 8

1. 255
2. 168
3. 361
4. 6300
5. 27 000
6. 200 000

7–10.
$$\frac{87}{27} + \frac{7}{9} \rightarrow 3$$
$$\frac{2}{3} + \frac{8}{24} \rightarrow 2$$
$$\frac{9}{7} + \frac{10}{14} \rightarrow 4$$
$$\frac{21}{8} + \frac{3}{8} \rightarrow 1$$

11. 75
12. 100 000
13. 180°
14. 2700
15. 92
16. 46 mm
17. 64 mm
18. 39 mm
19. 14.9 cm
20. $\frac{3}{4}$
21. $1\frac{1}{2}$
22. $2\frac{1}{4}$
23. 3
24. 3
25. 6
26. 8
27. parallelogram
28. kite
29. triangle (right-angled)
30. trapezium
31. pentagon
32. 840
33. $\frac{1}{15}$
34. 288
35. 120
36. 3
37. 5
38. 4
39. 10 cm²
40. 9 cm²
41. 8 cm²
42. 3 cm²
43. 144
44. 54
45. 102
46. 108
47. 9834.50
48. 274
49. 47.04
50. 50

Paper 9

1. 4820
2. 7517
3. 10 625
4. 9220
5. $9\frac{7}{12}$
6. $11\frac{1}{8}$
7. $7\frac{2}{7}$
8. $12\frac{1}{20}$

9. 1 h 40 min
10. 3
11. 24
12. 53
13. 14:06
14. 44.39
15. 48.16
16. 1.72
17. 14.6
18. 17
19. 19
20. 18
21. 4.23
22. 4.234

23–25.

26. rhombus
27. square
28. hexagon
29. 13.5
30. 20
31. 10
32. 1100
33. 135
34–35. 3, 7
36–37. 2, 7
38. 3
39. 3
40. 7
41. 5
42. 11
43. 13.05
44. 13.74
45. 14.25
46. 9.7
47. 3
48. $2\frac{1}{2}$ or 2.5
49. $2\frac{1}{4}$ or 2.25
50. 6

Paper 10

1. 1 in 6 or $\frac{1}{6}$
2. 1 in 2 or $\frac{1}{2}$
3. 1 in 3 or $\frac{1}{3}$
4. 1 in 2 or $\frac{1}{2}$
5. 1 in 3 or $\frac{1}{3}$
6. 1 in 6 or $\frac{1}{6}$
7. 11
8. 16

Bond Assessment Papers Maths 11+–12+ years Book 2

9   9
10   vertical
11   parallel
12   perpendicular
13   horizontal
14   £225.07
15   £9225
16   £7.92
17   £13.20
18   £6.50
19   £7.50
20   £6.25
21   1.5
22   119
23   0.75
24   107.35
25   $31\frac{11}{16}$
26   0.1575
27   5
28   2
29   4

30–32

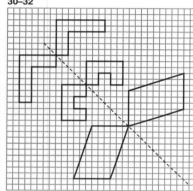

33   80
34   60
35   40
36   20
37   0
38   5
39   15
40   9
41   180
42   460
43   96
44   39
45   0.025
46   30°
47   40°
48   140°
49   300°
50   300°

Paper 11

1–4   11, 13, 17, 19
5   816
6   2096
7   176

8   424

9–14

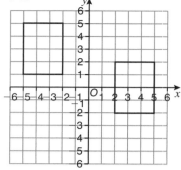

15–17   34, 106, 40
18   Aileen
19   Edward
20   25 seconds
21   40 seconds
22   55 seconds
23   £26.94
24   £41.19
25   £138.13
26   £14.25
27–30   2, 2, 3, 5
31   15
32   24
33   66
34   $\frac{3}{10}$
35   80
36   65
37   $\frac{4}{5}$

38–43

×	**0.2**	0.5	0.8
6	1.2	3.0	4.8
0.1	**0.02**	0.05	**0.08**
0.2	0.04	**0.1**	0.16

44   3
45   4
46   5
47   1.63 m
48   1.62 m
49   1.615 m
50   14 cm

Paper 12

1–6

	Two decimal places	One decimal place
4.1454	**4.15**	**4.1**
3.066	**3.07**	**3.1**
10.816	**10.82**	**10.8**

7   51
8   32
9   160

10   56
11   84
12   44
13–16   5040, 6750, 4149, 7758
17   50°
18   72.5°
19   45°
20   120°
21   0.24
22   0.285
23   0.315
24   0.355
25   0.115
26   0.03
27   6
28   16
29   8
30   10
31   $7\frac{1}{2}$ or 7.5
32   $4\frac{1}{2}$ or 4.5
33   $2\frac{1}{2}$ or 2.5
34   5
35   £356.95
36   £441.93
37   £8.06
38   £153.98
39   7
40   $\frac{1}{2}$
41   $\frac{1}{4}$
42   50
43   0.6
44   0.1

45–46

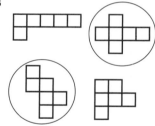

47   169.31
48   261.14
49   12.95
50   7.6

Paper 13

1   2
2   4
3   6
4   8
5   3
6   30
7   28
8   32
9   28
10   34
11   26

A4

12 F
13 $\frac{1}{8}$
14 $\frac{1}{2}$
15 $\frac{3}{8}$
16 $\frac{1}{2}$
17–18

19 5
20 5
21 8
22 8
23 6
24 12
25–29

14	19	12
13	15	17
18	11	16

30 $5(m + n)$ or $5m + 5n$
31–37

y
12
11
10
9
8
7
6
5
4
3
2
1
O 1 2 3 4 5 6 7 8 9 10 11 12 x

38 1
39 5
40 7
41 18
42 11
43 6 753 450
44 6 753 400
45 6 753 000
46 6 750 000
47 6 800 000
48 7 000 000
49 $8\frac{1}{2}$ or 8.5
50 $10\frac{1}{2}$ or 10.5

Paper 14

1 11.38
2 18.21
3 22.82
4 25.16
5 $\frac{16}{20}$
6 $\frac{20}{25}$

7 $\frac{20}{28}$
8 $\frac{25}{35}$
9 7
10 3
11 5
12 33
13 $\frac{1}{2}$
14 $\frac{1}{6}$
15 $\frac{1}{3}$
16 48°
17 acute
18 140°
19 obtuse
20 324°
21 reflex
22 70
23 28
24 42
25 area is doubled
26 area is doubled
27 area is four times greater
28 area is the same
29 area is six times greater
30 -5 or $\div 3.5$
31 $\div 3$
32 9
33 4.35 cm
34 3.6 cm
35 4.9 cm
36 $12\frac{1}{8}$
37 $14\frac{4}{9}$
38 $8\frac{1}{5}$
39 $12\frac{1}{2}$
40 $8\frac{2}{21}$
41 7
42 65
43 26
44 39
45 £552.50
46 £97.50
47 £22.20
48 £5.55
49 £62.55
50 £6.95

Paper 15

1 33
2 15
3 one hundred and twenty-three million, four hundred and fifty-six thousand, seven hundred and eighty-nine
4 Ali
5 20
6 67
7 23
8 34

9 4
10 5
11 3
12 49
13 16 460
14 1050
15 483
16 72
17–20 $\frac{2}{3}, \frac{3}{4}, \frac{5}{6}, \frac{7}{8}$
21 1.65
22 2
23 $2\frac{1}{8}$
24 $2\frac{5}{8}$
25 48%
26 36%
27 16%
28 22.75
29 20
30 28.8
31 22.4
32 19.38
33 17.8
34–39

Mercury			
50 300 000	Venus		
91 700 000	41 400 000	Earth	
170 000 000	119 700 000	78 300 000	Mars

40–43 15 633, 20 709, 35 172, 40 365
44–46

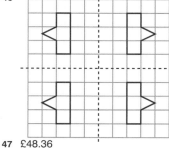

47 £48.36
48 £129.12
49 £158.22
50 £345.93

Paper 16

1 £50.55
2 £521.10
3 £363.60
4 £502.50
5 $8a^2 + 2b$ or $2(4a^2 + b)$
6 $3x^2 - 4y$
7 $11p^2 - p$ or $p(11p - 1)$
8 $4ab - 4a$ or $4(ab - a)$ or $4a(b - 1)$
9 18
10 6
11 23
12 20

13 106.5
14 0.75
15 90°
16 120°
17 45°
18 360°
19 180°

20–25

	Length	Breadth	Area	Perimeter
Rectangle A	8.5 cm	6 cm	**51 cm²**	**29 cm**
Rectangle B	9 cm	**4.5 cm**	40.5 cm²	**27 cm**
Rectangle C	7.5 cm	**5.5 cm**	**41.25 cm²**	26 cm

26 $2\frac{1}{6}$
27 $2\frac{1}{2}$
28 $5\frac{1}{8}$
29 $5\frac{5}{8}$
30 $11\frac{7}{10}$
31 12

32–37

Square — A rectangle with four equal sides

Parallelogram — A quadrilateral with equal and parallel opposite sides

Kite — A quadrilateral with two pairs of equal adjacent sides

Rhombus — A parallelogram with four equal sides

Trapezium — A quadrilateral with one pair of opposite sides that are parallel

Rectangle — A quadrilateral with four right angles and equal opposite sides

38 <
39 =
40 >
41 >
42 <
43 $\frac{1}{16}$
44 $\frac{1}{4}$
45 $\frac{3}{8}$
46 $\frac{3}{16}$
47 $\frac{1}{8}$
48 4
49 0.7
50 4

Paper 17

1 15.27
2 861.9
3 18.98
4 785.9
5 3.1
6 22.95
7 12
8 24
9 10
10 48
11 15 168
12 18 256
13 10 216
14–17 $\frac{1}{5}$, $\frac{1}{4}$, $\frac{3}{8}$, $\frac{1}{2}$
18 0.1046
19 2.5735
20 0.9064
21 0.0137
22 13
23 23
24 43
25 53
26 7.5
27 4.5
28 6

29–34

Stamps per bag	32	33	34	35	36	37
Tally	I	⅃⅂⅂⅂ II	⅃⅂⅂⅂ III	⅃⅂⅂⅂ IIII	IIII	I
Frequency	1	7	8	9	4	1

35 90
36 63
37 30
38 96
39 752.85 m
40 1613.56 m
41 555.5 m
42 102 m

43–45

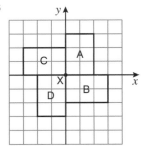

46 (−1, −1.5)
47 (−1.5, 1)
48 (0, 2)
49 (1.5, 1)
50 (1, −1.5)

Paper 18

1 £10.33
2 £32.02
3 £18.24
4 £20.20
5 £38.77
6 9
7 9
8 8
9 9
10 parallel
11 perpendicular
12 horizontal
13 vertical
14 perpendicular
15 £31.20
16 £35.35
17 £47.35
18 A 1.8
19 B 3.6
20 C 6.2
21 D 5.4
22 $\frac{1}{7}$
23 $\frac{2}{7}$
24 $\frac{1}{14}$
25 $\frac{5}{14}$
26 $\frac{9}{14}$
27 $\frac{3}{7}$
28 <
29 >
30 <
31 =
32 >
33 +
34 ÷
35 ×
36 −
37 112 m²
38 16 m²
39 80 m²
40–44 123 × 76
45 38°
46 128°
47 4
48 7
49 3
50 20

Paper 19

1 23
2 38
3 45
4 90
5 82

A6

6 61

7 £18.09

8 £475.48

9 £84.00

10 £24.02

11 £12.15

12 4.89

13 7.52

14 6.89

15 6.38

16 35°

17 acute

18 132°

19 obtuse

20 320°

21 reflex

22 7

23 12

24 7

25–29 −7.2, −3.6, −2.7, 2.9, 4.1

30 38 mins

31 35 mins

32 35 mins

33 19 mins

34 30

35 18

36 80

37 48

38 45

39 20

40 15

41 25

42–47

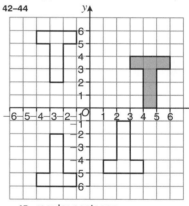

48–50

Paper 20

1 12

2 11

3 7

4 20

5 3600

6 168

7 720

8 $4\frac{3}{10}$

9 $2\frac{1}{2}$

10 $14\frac{1}{9}$

11 20%

12 50%

13 70%

14 25%

15 30%

16 B

17 54

18 2.38

19 12 (or 10.5)

20 0.25

21 £10.41

22 £2.30

23 £1.32

24 £1.60

25 2.88 m²

26 2.9 m²

27 1.375 m²

28 $\frac{1}{2}$

29 $\frac{9}{16}$

30 $\frac{7}{12}$

31 $\frac{5}{8}$

32 $\frac{4}{6}$

33 261

34 405

35 273

36 369

37 £72

38 £45

39 £135

40 £54

41 $\frac{1}{6}$

42 $\frac{1}{2}$

43 $\frac{2}{3}$

44 0

45 1

46 $10a − 4$ or $2(5a − 2)$

47 $5x^2 + 3$

48 $2p + 2q$ or $2(p + q)$

49 $3z + 5y$

50 $2a^2 − 7b$

Paper 21

1 24.5

2 71.25

3 9.73

---

4 42.9

5 42

6 48.5

7 14

8 35.7

9–13 −1.25, −0.75, −0.5, 1.25, 1.5

14 8

15 11

16 14

17–20 2, 3, 3, 5

21–22 3, 5

23 1 h 50 min

24 £38

25 £7.15

26 isosceles

27 75

28 scalene

29 17

30 right-angled

31 56

32 3.6 (3.575)

33 1.1 (1.135)

34 5.6

35 £30.54

36 £108.45

37 £6

38 £50.16

39 −2.25

40 −4.7

41 −36

42–44

45 regular pentagon

46 regular octagon

47 kite

48 90 cm³

49 150 cm³

50 87.75 cm³

Paper 22

1 672

2 27

3 214 563

4 398 762

5 6

6 $\frac{1}{2}$

7 $\frac{1}{26}$
8 $\frac{1}{52}$
9 $\frac{1}{4}$
10–13 A, F, G, J
14–15 5, 7
16–17 11, 13
18–19 17, 19
20 1
21 1
22 3
23 8
24 2
25 5
26 $\frac{1}{18}$
27 $1\frac{1}{8}$
28 $12\frac{23}{70}$
29 $12\frac{5}{54}$
30 $8\frac{1}{2}$
31 2.5
32 3.75
33 2.25
34 3
35 3
36 4
37 7
38 14
39 19
40 0
41 ÷
42 −
43 +
44 ×
45 288
46 747.6
47 4.956
48 1.087
49 410
50 301

Paper 23

1 13.5
2 4.6
3 14.75
4 35.5
5 10
6 14
7 28

8 32
9 <
10 =
11 >
12 <
13 >
14 20 °C
15 19 °C
16 19.5 °C
17 8 °C
18–19 3, 9
20–21 2, 4
22 5
23 20
24 9
25 1
26 $-\frac{5}{7}$
27 $-\frac{3}{8}$
28 $-\frac{2}{7}$
29 $\frac{1}{32}$
30 $\frac{1}{16}$
31 334 cm²
32 558 cm²
33 288 cm²
34 98 cm
35 168 cm
36 124 cm
37 300
38 −20
39 0.4
40 72
41 10
42 76
43 455
44 6
45 8
46 9
47 5
48 4
49 2
50 6

Paper 24

1 198
2 513
3 396
4 1089

5 1170
6 <
7 >
8 =
9 >
10 <

11–13

14–19

Length	Breadth	Perimeter	Area
16 cm	9 cm	**50 cm**	**144** cm²
14 cm	**8 cm**	44 cm	**112** cm²
13 cm	**7 cm**	**40 cm**	91 cm²

20 72 cm²
21 54 cm²
22 24 cm²
23 216 cm²
24 60
25 55
26 72.5
27 8100
28 4508
29 4864
30 25 088

31–35

36 76
37 38
38 96
39 32
40 3
41 $\frac{1}{3}$
42 2
43 $1\frac{1}{2}$
44 7
45 11
46 3
47 5
48 7
49 11
50 13

Calculate the areas and perimeters of these shapes.

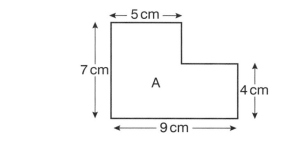

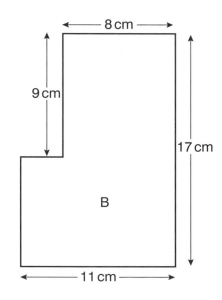

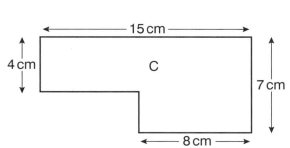

B 20

7–8 Shape A has an area of _____ cm² and a perimeter of _____ cm.

9–10 Shape B has an area of _____ cm² and a perimeter of _____ cm.

11–12 Shape C has an area of _____ cm² and a perimeter of _____ cm.

6

13–16 The digits in multiples of 9 sum to 9 through repeated addition.
For example, $633 \times 9 = 5697$, $5 + 6 + 9 + 7 = 27$ and $2 + 7 = 9$. Use this fact to identify which of the numbers below are divisible by 9. Circle those that are.

5040   3009   6750   4049   4149   7758

B2/B3

4

Work out the size of each of the marked angles in these shapes.

B17/B18
B 20

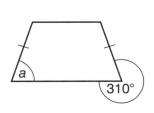
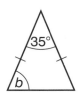
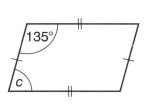
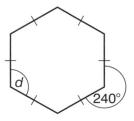

17 Angle $a =$ _____

18 Angle $b =$ _____

19 Angle $c =$ _____

20 Angle $d =$ _____

4

Write the numbers indicated by the arrows.

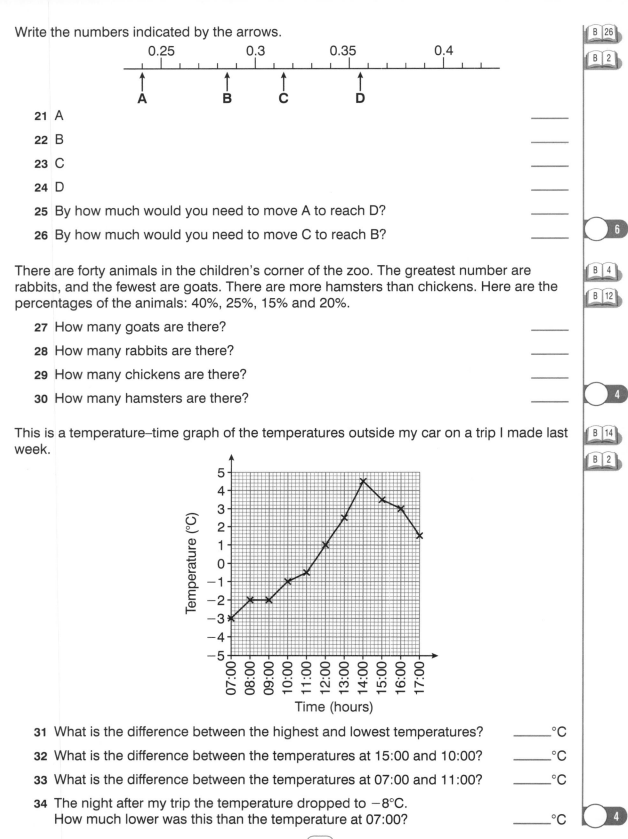

21 A _____

22 B _____

23 C _____

24 D _____

25 By how much would you need to move A to reach D? _____

26 By how much would you need to move C to reach B? _____

6

There are forty animals in the children's corner of the zoo. The greatest number are rabbits, and the fewest are goats. There are more hamsters than chickens. Here are the percentages of the animals: 40%, 25%, 15% and 20%.

27 How many goats are there? _____

28 How many rabbits are there? _____

29 How many chickens are there? _____

30 How many hamsters are there? _____

4

This is a temperature–time graph of the temperatures outside my car on a trip I made last week.

31 What is the difference between the highest and lowest temperatures? _____°C

32 What is the difference between the temperatures at 15:00 and 10:00? _____°C

33 What is the difference between the temperatures at 07:00 and 11:00? _____°C

34 The night after my trip the temperature dropped to −8°C.
How much lower was this than the temperature at 07:00? _____°C

4

Ms Brown has to buy furniture for some offices. Here is the price list for some of the items that she looked at.

Desk	£79.98
Bookcase	£49.99
Cupboard	£76.99
Filing cabinet	£159.99
Desk chair	£109.99
Visitor chair	£34.99
Wastepaper bin	£6.99

B 2
B 3
B 12

35 She buys a desk, wastepaper bin, filing cabinet and desk chair for one office. How much did that cost? _____

36 For another office she buys all of the items listed above except the cupboard. How much was that? _____

37 She needs six more wastepaper bins. How much change would she get for these from £50? _____

38 If she buys four cupboards she gets a 50% discount. How much will she pay for the four cupboards? _____

Find the length of one side of each square.

39 Area = 49 sq in _____ in

40 Area = $\frac{1}{4}$ sq ft _____ ft

41 Area = $\frac{1}{16}$ sq in _____ in

42 Area = 2500 sq yd _____ yd

43 Area = 0.36 sq cm _____ cm

44 Area = 0.01 sq km _____ km

45–46 Circle the nets that will fold to make a closed cube.

Calculate the answers to these.

47 0.53 + 103.7 + 65.08 = _____

48 237.5 + 2.86 + 20.78 = _____

49 8.17 + 3.65 + 1.13 = _____

50 4.2 + 3.15 + 0.25 = _____

B 20
B 21
B 11

Now go to the Progress Chart to record your score! Total 50

Paper 13

Using only the digits 2, 3, 4, 6 and 8, find the values of A, B, C, D and E. Use the expressions below to help you.

$$A + B = C$$
$$A \times B = D$$
$$C \div 2 = E$$
$$(C + B) - A = D$$

1 A = _____

2 B = _____

3 C = _____

4 D = _____

5 E = _____

6–11 Find the price per metre of these six different rolls of sticky tape.

Tape	Length of tape	Price of roll	Price/metre
A	11.0 m	£3.30	_____ p
B	12.5 m	£3.50	_____ p
C	14.5 m	£4.64	_____ p
D	20.5 m	£5.74	_____ p
E	16.5 m	£5.61	_____ p
F	19.0 m	£4.94	_____ p

12 Which is the best buy?   Tape _____

I spin this octagonal spinner. Work out the probabilities to answer the questions below. Write your answers as fractions in their **lowest terms**.

What is the probability of getting:

13 a 6? _____

14 an odd number? _____

15 a number greater than 5? _____

16 a number less than 5? _____

17–18 Circle the shapes that when rotated through 180° will fit exactly on the starting position.

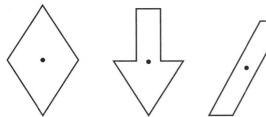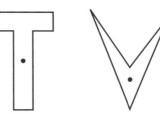

B 24

2

How many faces, **vertices** and **edges** does the square-based pyramid have?

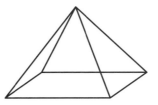

B 21

19 Faces = _____

20 Vertices = _____

21 Edges = _____

If I stick two identical square-based pyramids together, base to base, how many faces, **vertices** and **edges** are there?

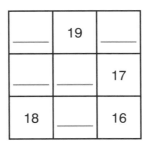

22 Faces = _____

23 Vertices = _____

24 Edges = _____

6

25–29 All the rows, columns and diagonals in this square sum to 45. Using the numbers 11–15 inclusive, complete the square. Each number can only be used once.

B 2

_____	19	_____
_____	_____	17
18	_____	16

5

30 Every day Ranji spends *m* pence on a bus ticket to take her to school. She walks home, but spends *n* pence on sweets every day. In five days, how much does she spend?
Write your answer as an expression.   _____

B 8

1

31–35 Plot these **coordinates** and draw the shape that they define.
(1, 9), (3, 9), (1, 10), (3, 10), (2, 11)

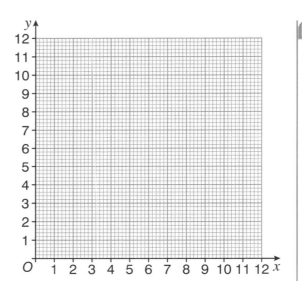

B 23

36 Translate and draw the pentagon 6 units right and 2 units down.

37 Translate this second pentagon 5 units to the left and 3 units down. Draw a third pentagon there.

38–39 Starting at the first pentagon, how many units to the right and how many units down is the third pentagon?

Units right _____   Units down _____

9

B2/B3

40 I think of a number, subtract 2.8 and multiply by 3. The answer is 12.6.
What was the number that I was thinking of?   _____

41 I think of a number, add 3.6 and multiply by 2. The answer is 43.2.
What was the number that I was thinking of?   _____

42 I think of a number, subtract 2.5 and divide by 5. The answer is 1.7.
What was the number that I was thinking of?   _____

3

43–48 Complete this table.

B 1

Start	To nearest 10	To nearest 100	To nearest 1000	To nearest 10 000	To nearest 100 000	To nearest 1 000 000
6 753 449	_____	_____	_____	_____	_____	_____

6

B 8

49 $(A + B + C) \div 3 = 8$. If $C = 7$, what is $(A + B) \div 2$?   _____

50 $(X + Y + Z) \div 3 = 12$. If $X = 15$, what is $(Y + Z) \div 2$?   _____

2

Calculate the answers to these decimal subtractions.

B 14

   1 $43.12 - 31.74 =$ _____

   2 $72.56 - 54.35 =$ _____

   3 $89.74 - 66.92 =$ _____

   4 $56.43 - 31.27 =$ _____

4

Continue these sequences.

B7/B10

5–6 $\frac{4}{5}$ $\frac{8}{10}$ $\frac{12}{15}$ _____   _____

7–8 $\frac{5}{7}$ $\frac{10}{14}$ $\frac{15}{21}$ _____   _____

4

Find the values that a, b and c represent in these.

B8/B6

   9 $a^2 - 13 = 36$ $a =$ _____

  10 $b^3 + 5 = 32$ $b =$ _____

  11 $28 - 4c = 8$ $c =$ _____

Using the values of a, b and c above, work out the value of:

  12 $4a + 5b - 2c =$ _____

4

In a bag of marbles there are 9 red marbles, 6 blue marbles and 3 white marbles. Using fractions in their **lowest terms**, calculate the probability of drawing out:

B16/B10

  13 a red marble. _____

  14 a white marble. _____

  15 a blue marble. _____

3

Calculate the marked angles and identify each type of angle using the terms **obtuse**, **reflex** and **acute**.

B 17

16–17 Angle a measures _____   Angle type _____

18–19 Angle b measures _____   Angle type _____

20–21 Angle c measures _____   Angle type _____

6

Angus bought some new canes to use on his allotment. He bought 3 metre canes, $2\frac{1}{2}$ metre canes, and 2 metre canes in the ratio of 5 : 3 : 2. He bought 140 canes in total.

B 13

22 How many 3 m canes did he buy? _____

23 How many 2 m canes did he buy? _____

24 How many $2\frac{1}{2}$ m canes did he buy? _____

3

What happens to the area of a rectangle:

B 20

25 if the length is doubled? _____

26 if the breadth is doubled? _____

27 if both length and breadth are doubled? _____

28 if length is doubled and breadth halved? _____

29 if length is doubled and breadth tripled? _____

5

30–32 Write in the missing elements in these function machines.

B 9

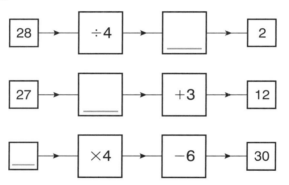

3

Use the perimeters of these regular shapes to find the lengths of the sides.

B 20

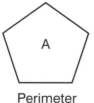

Perimeter
= 21.75 cm

Perimeter
= 21.6 cm

Perimeter
= 14.7 cm

33 The length of each side of A is _____

34 The length of each side of B is _____

35 The length of each side of C is _____

3

Solve these **mixed number** problems giving your answers in their **lowest terms**.

36 $5\frac{1}{2} + 6\frac{5}{8} =$ _____

37 $7\frac{7}{9} + 6\frac{2}{3} =$ _____

38 $15\frac{4}{5} - 7\frac{9}{15} =$ _____

39 $21\frac{1}{6} - 8\frac{12}{18} =$ _____

40 $12\frac{20}{21} - 4\frac{6}{7} =$ _____

5

In mathematics, where brackets are not used, we always carry out operations in the order ÷ and × first, then + and −, working from left to right. Use this fact to calculate the right answers to these.

41 $6 + 21 \div 7 - 2 =$ _____

42 $48 - 13 + 5 \times 6 =$ _____

43 $3 \times 8 + 6 \div 2 - 1 =$ _____

44 $27 - 12 \div 4 + 15 =$ _____

4

Ms Baht has bought some of this office equipment. The full prices are shown below.

£650

£27.75

£69.50

The computer has a 15% discount.

45 What is its sale price? _____

46 What is the saving? _____

The calculator has a 20% discount.

47 What is its sale price? _____

48 What is the saving? _____

The telephone pack has a 10% discount.

49 What is its sale price? _____

50 What is the saving? _____

6

Now go to the Progress Chart to record your score!   **Total**   50

Paper 15

1 Party poppers come in boxes of 8. How many boxes do you need for a street party of 264 people? _____

2 The black, white and grey crayons make up 20% of a set of colours. How many colours are in the set altogether? _____

3 Write in words 123 456 789. _____

4 Sam got 190 out of 250 in a test and Ali got 64 out of 80 in a similar test. Who did better? _____

4

Calculate the following as whole percentages. Round up or down as necessary.

5 24 out of 120 _____%

6 18 out of 27 _____%

7 14 out of 60 _____%

8 12 out of 35 _____%

Work out the values of x, y and z in these expressions.

9 $x^2 - 8 = 8$ $x =$ _____

10 $7 + 3y = 22$ $y =$ _____

11 $z^2 - 10 = -1$ $z =$ _____

Use the values you have found for x, y and z to solve this.

12 $2x^2 + xy - z =$ _____

Change these measures to millilitres.

13 16.46 litres = _____ ml

14 1.05 litres = _____ ml

15 0.483 litres = _____ ml

16 0.072 litres = _____ ml

17–20 Put these fractions in order from smallest to largest.

$\frac{7}{8}$ $\frac{2}{3}$ $\frac{5}{6}$ $\frac{3}{4}$

_____   _____   _____   _____

Continue these sequences.

21–22 0.6   0.95   1.3   _____   _____

23–24 $\frac{5}{8}$ $1\frac{1}{8}$ $1\frac{5}{8}$ _____   _____

There are 12 green cubes, 9 blue cubes and 4 white cubes in a bag. Write the probability of pulling out each colour as a percentage.

25 A green cube   _____

26 A blue cube   _____

27 A white cube   _____

Calculate the area and perimeter of each of these rectangles.

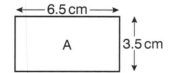
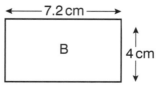
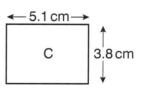

28–29 Rectangle A has an area of _____ cm² and a perimeter of _____ cm.

44

30–31 Rectangle B has an area of _____ cm² and a perimeter of _____ cm.

32–33 Rectangle C has an area of _____ cm² and a perimeter of _____ cm.

6

B 14

B 2

34–39

Planet	Distance from the Sun in kilometres
Mercury	57 900 000
Venus	108 200 000
Earth	149 600 000
Mars	227 900 000

The table above shows the distances of the inner planets from the Sun. Use the data to complete the distance below.

Mercury			
_____	Venus		
_____	_____	Earth	
_____	_____	_____	Mars

6

40–43 The digits in multiples of 9 sum to 9 through repeated addition. For example, $750 \times 9 = 6750$, $6 + 7 + 5 + 0 = 18$, and $1 + 8 = 9$. Use this fact to identify which of these numbers can be exactly divided by 9. Circle those that can.

39 254   15 633   20 709   65 027   35 172   12 589   40 365

B 2

4

44–46 Draw all the reflections of this shape using these mirror lines which are at right angles to each other.

B 24

3

47–50 These items are all on sale with one third off. What was the full price of each?

B 10

Sale price	Original full price
£32.24	_____
£86.08	_____
£105.48	_____
£230.62	_____

4

Now go to the Progress Chart to record your score!   **Total**   50

Paper 16

Calculate the answers to these money multiplication problems.

B 25

1 £16.85 × 3 = _____   **2** £104.22 × 5 = _____

3 £90.90 × 4 = _____   **4** £83.75 × 6 = _____

4

Simplify these expressions.

B 8

5 $6a^2 + 2a^2 + 3b - b =$ _____   **6** $4x^2 - 7y + 3y - x^2 =$ _____

7 $3p^2 - 5p + 8p^2 + 4p =$ _____   **8** $7ab - 6a + 2a - 3ab =$ _____

4

Find the **mode** and **range** of each of these sets of numbers.

B 15

9–10 18 16 15 14 18 20 19 17 18   **Mode** = _____   **Range** = _____

11–12 5 12 23 18 25 23 17 6 11   **Mode** = _____   **Range** = _____

13–14 106.5 106.25 107 106.5 106.25 106.5   **Mode** = _____   **Range** = _____

6

Look at these shapes and then state how many degrees they have to be rotated through before each fits exactly on the starting position.

B 24
B 17

A   B   C   D   E

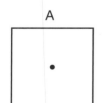 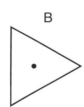 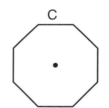  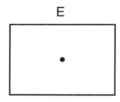

15 Shape A _____   **16** Shape B _____

17 Shape C _____   **18** Shape D _____

19 Shape E _____

5

20–25 Complete this table of dimensions.

B 20

	Length	Breadth	Area	Perimeter
Rectangle A	8.5 cm	6 cm	_____ cm²	_____ cm
Rectangle B	9 cm	_____ cm	40.5 cm²	_____ cm
Rectangle C	7.5 cm	_____ cm	_____ cm²	26 cm

6

Put the missing numbers in these sequences.

26–27 $1\frac{2}{3}$ $1\frac{5}{6}$ 2   _____ $2\frac{1}{3}$ _____

28–29 $4\frac{5}{8}$ $4\frac{7}{8}$ _____ $5\frac{3}{8}$ _____

30–31 $10\frac{4}{5}$ $11\frac{1}{10}$ $11\frac{2}{5}$ _____   _____

32–37 Draw lines to connect each shape to its description.

Square	A **parallelogram** with four equal sides
Parallelogram	A quadrilateral with four right angles and equal opposite sides
Kite	A rectangle with four equal sides
Rhombus	A quadrilateral with one pair of opposite sides that are parallel
Trapezium	A quadrilateral with two pairs of equal adjacent sides
Rectangle	A quadrilateral with equal and parallel opposite sides

Insert the symbols $<$, $>$ or $=$ as appropriate.

38 $12^2 - 100$ _____ 5×9

39 6×2^2 _____ $3 \times 2 \times 4$

40 $2^3 \times 2^2$ _____ $2 \times 2 \times 2 \times 3$

41 $5^2 + 4^2$ _____ $2 \times 4 \times 5$

42 $2^2 \times 2^2$ _____ $6^2 - 2^2$

On a recent expedition to some lakes and marshes the village bird-watching club counted these numbers of five varieties of water birds.

Answer each question using fractions in the **lowest terms**.

43 What fraction were grebes? _____

44 What fraction were shovelers? _____

45 What fraction were teal? _____

46 What fraction were moorhens? _____

47 What fraction were oystercatchers? _____

8 grebes

24 moorhens

32 shovelers

16 oyster-catchers

48 teal

Put in the missing numbers.

48 $0.4 \times$ _____ $= 1.6$

49 _____ $\times 8 = 5.6$

50 $3.2 \times$ _____ $= 12.8$

B 7
B 10
6
B 19
6
A6/B2
B6/B3
5
B 14
B 10
5
B 11
3

Paper 17

Solve these decimal problems.

1 $7.39 + 7.88 =$ _____

2 $863 - 1.1 =$ _____

3 $3.1 + 15.88 =$ _____

4 $795 - 9.1 =$ _____

5 $65.1 \div 21 =$ _____

6 $7.65 \times 3 =$ _____

What is the **lowest common multiple** of each pair of numbers?

7 4 and 6 _____

8 8 and 6 _____

9 5 and 10 _____

10 12 and 16 _____

11–13 A number is divisible by 8 if the last three digits are divisible by 8. Underline the numbers here that are divisible by 8.

15 168   14 204   18 256   10 216   11 318   12 284

14–17 Put these fractions in order from smallest to largest.

$\frac{3}{8}$ $\frac{1}{2}$ $\frac{1}{4}$ $\frac{1}{5}$

_____   _____   _____   _____

Change these measures to kilograms.

18 $104.6 \, g =$ _____ kg

19 $2573.5 \, g =$ _____ kg

20 $906.4 \, g =$ _____ kg

21 $13.7 \, g =$ _____ kg

22–25 Circle the **prime numbers**.

13   23   33   43   53   63

B 25

6

B 5

4

B 3

3

B 10

4

B 25

4

B 6

4

Calculate the areas of the triangles shown here. Scale: each square on the grid is 1 cm². B 18

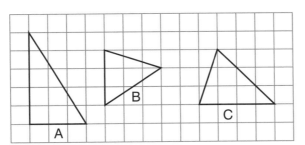

26 Triangle A = _____ cm²

27 Triangle B = _____ cm²

28 Triangle C = _____ cm²   **3**

29–34 Mr Hodgkins sells bags of old stamps. He puts about 35 stamps in each bag. The B 14
table below shows the actual number of stamps contained in a sample of 30 bags.

35	34	33	35	33
33	34	35	35	36
34	33	35	35	35
36	33	34	34	34
35	34	33	32	33
37	35	34	36	36

Using the given data, complete this frequency table.

Stamps per bag	32	33	34	35	36	37
Tally						
Frequency						

6

Calculate these percentages.   B 12

35 25% of 360 = _____

36 15% of 420 = _____

37 12% of 250 = _____

38 32% of 300 = _____   **4**

49

Calculate the answers to these measures problems, giving your answers in metres.

39 35 cm + 0.75 km + 2.5 m = _____

40 1.6 km + 13.4 m + 16 cm = _____

41 (750 m + 306 m) − (50 cm + 0.5 km) = _____

42 (36 m × 3) − (150 cm × 4) = _____

B25/B2 B 3 4 B 23 B 17

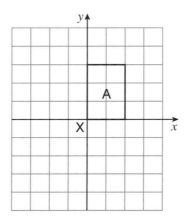

Rotate rectangle A about origin X through each of the amounts given below. Draw and label it in its new grid position each time.

43 90° clockwise (rectangle B)

44 90° anticlockwise (rectangle C)

45 180° anticlockwise (rectangle D)

3

Write the **coordinates** for the **vertices** of this pentagon.

B 23

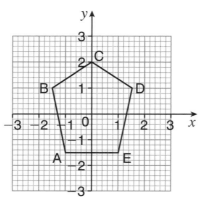

46 A _____   **47** B _____   **48** C _____

49 D _____   **50** E _____

5

Paper 18

Solve these money problems. Give your answers in pounds.

B 1
B 2

1. 406p + 627p = _____
2. 603p + £25.99 = _____
3. £98.99 − £80.75 = _____
4. £15.15 + 505p = _____
5. £32.50 + 627p = _____

5

Two dice were rolled 12 times. Here are the total scores.

B 15

3   12   10   4   6   9   11   9   9   11   4   8

6. What is the **mode**? _____
7. What is the **median**? _____
8. What is the **mean**? _____
9. What is the **range**? _____

4

B 17

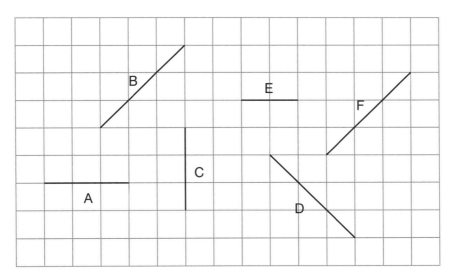

Using the terms parallel, perpendicular, horizontal and vertical, complete these statements.

10. A is _____ to E
11. D is _____ to F
12. E is a _____ line
13. C is a _____ line
14. B is _____ to D

5

This table shows the cost of posting parcels to the Republic of Ireland.

Up to 0.5 kg	£6.60
Up to 1.0 kg	£8.05
Up to 1.5 kg	£9.50
Up to 2.0 kg	£10.95
Up to 2.5 kg	£12.40
Up to 3.0 kg	£13.65
Up to 3.5 kg	£14.90
Up to 4.0 kg	£16.15
Up to 4.5 kg	£17.40

Three people came into our local post office to send a variety of parcels. What did each person pay?

15 Three parcels weighing 0.4 kg, 2.6 kg and 1.7 kg _____

16 Three parcels weighing 0.6 kg, 2.3 kg and 3.5 kg _____

17 Four parcels weighing 300 g, 1.9 kg, 2.5 kg and 4.1 kg _____

3

18–21 Put the missing output numbers (A and C) and the missing input numbers (B and D) in this function machine.

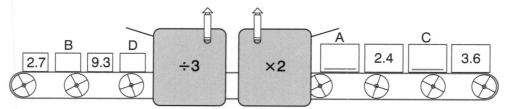

4

Ms Price wrote MISSISSIPPI MUD on a strip of paper and then cut the strip to make separate letters. She shuffled them on a table, face down. Writing your answers in the **lowest terms**, what are the chances of her turning over:

22 a letter M? _____

23 a letter S? _____

24 a letter D? _____

25 a vowel? _____

26 a consonant? _____

27 a letter I or P? _____

6

Put the symbols $<$, $>$ or $=$ in these statements. Remember, calculate what is inside brackets first.

28 1.5×3.5 _____ $11 \div 2$

29 $4.8 \div 4$ _____ $0.65 + 0.45$

30 $(6 \times 3.5) \div 7$ _____ $6.4 \div 2$

31 7.25×3 _____ $87 \div 4$

32 $3.4 + 16.25$ _____ $58.8 \div 3$

A 6
B 3
B 11

5

Put the missing operators $+$, $-$, $\times$ or $\div$ in these.

33 266 _____ $38 = 304$

34 266 _____ $38 = 7$

35 266 _____ $38 = 10\,108$

36 266 _____ $38 = 228$

B 2
B 3

4

This is a map of a garden that has two square flower beds, and the paths are all 2 m wide.

B 20

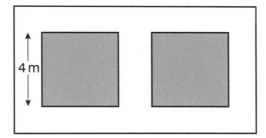

37 What is the area of the whole garden? _____

38 What is the area of each of the flower beds? _____

39 What is the area of the path? _____

3

40–44 Put the digits 1, 2, 3, 6 and 7 in the boxes to make the calculation correct.

☐ ☐ ☐ $\times$ ☐ ☐ $= 9348$

B 3
5

Use your protractor to measure these angles to the nearest 1°.

B 26

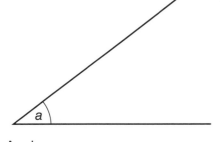

45 Angle $a =$ _____   **46** Angle $b =$ _____

2

Find the values of x, y and z in these expressions.

47 $x^2 - 9 = 7$ $x =$ _____   B 8

48 $4y + 9 = 37$ $y =$ _____   B 6

49 $21 - z^2 = 12$ $z =$ _____

Use the values you have found for x, y and z to solve this.

50 $3x + 2y - 2z =$ _____   4

Now go to the Progress Chart to record your score!   Total   50

Paper 19

Complete these sequences.   B 7

1–2	8	12	17	_____	30	_____	47
3–4	15	20	30	_____	65	_____	120
5–6	106	99	91	_____	72	_____	49

6

Work out these fractions.   B 10

7 Half of £36.18   _____

8 Half of £950.96   _____

9 Three-quarters of £112   _____

10 A quarter of £96.08   _____

11 A third of £36.45   _____

5

B 3
B 2

Large letter (353 mm × 250 mm)	Weight	First class postage
A	0–100 g	44p
B	101 g–250 g	65p
C	251 g–500 g	90p
D	501 g–750 g	131p

This table shows the costs of first class post for large letters.

The table below shows the large letters posted by four people in the village yesterday.

	A	B	C	D
Ms Brown	2	0	3	1
Mr Henry	0	2	4	2
Mrs Barnes	1	3	5	0
Mr Joseph	0	1	2	3

12 How much did Ms Brown pay? £ _____

13 How much did Mr Henry pay? £ _____

14 How much did Mrs Barnes pay? £ _____

15 How much did Mr Joseph pay? £ _____

B 26
B 17

Use your protractor (and the terms **obtuse**, **acute** and **reflex**) to find and name these angles. Measure the angles to the nearest 1°.

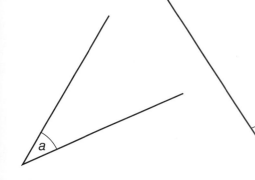

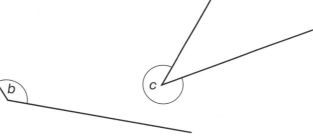

16–17 Angle *a* measures _____   Angle type _____

18–19 Angle *b* measures _____   Angle type _____

20–21 Angle *c* measures _____   Angle type _____

Look at the given shape, then answer the questions.

B 21

22 How many faces?   _____

23 How many **edges**?   _____

24 How many **vertices**?   _____

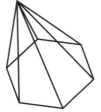

25–29 Put these in order, least first.

-2.7   4.1   2.9   -3.6   -7.2

_____   _____   _____   _____   _____

B 6

A student teacher was asked to watch a mathematics lesson and determine how many minutes the children spent working. The results were:

43   29   28   31   38   45   27   38   32   44   26   35   38   42   29

B 15

30 What is the **mode**? _____

31 What is the **median**? _____

32 What is the **mean**? _____

33 What is the **range**? _____

4

What are the lowest numbers that the following will divide exactly into?

B 5

34 6 and 10 _____

35 6 and 9 _____

36 10 and 16 _____

37 12 and 16 _____

38 3 and 5 and 9 _____

5

In the school garden Winston, Sam and Chris grew carrots. They pulled up 60 carrots and shared them out in the ratio of their families. Winston lives in a family of four, Sam in a family of three and Chris in a family of five.

B 13

How many carrots did:

39 Winston receive? _____

40 Sam receive? _____

41 Chris receive? _____

3

B 26

B 4

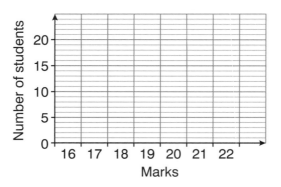

42–47 Draw a bar chart to show these results in a recent music examination.

2 students got 17   5 students got 16

7 students got 19   9 students got 18

14 students got 22   18 students got 20

6

48–50 Reflect these shapes in the mirror line.

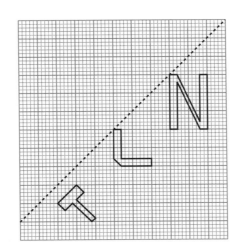

B 24

3

Now go to the Progress Chart to record your score! **Total** 50

Paper 20

What are the **square roots** of each of these?

1 $\sqrt{144}$ _____

2 $\sqrt{121}$ _____

3 $\sqrt{49}$ _____

4 $\sqrt{400}$ _____

B 6

4

5 How many seconds are there in an hour? _____ seconds

6 How many hours in a week? _____ hours

7 How many hours are there in June? _____ hours

B 27

3

Calculate the answers to these fraction problems giving answers in the **lowest terms**.

8 $1\frac{3}{5} + 2\frac{7}{10} =$ _____

9 $5\frac{6}{8} - 3\frac{1}{4} =$ _____

10 $6\frac{4}{9} + 7\frac{2}{3} =$ _____

B 10

3

A

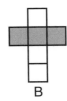

B

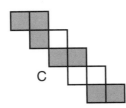

C

D

E

What percentage of each shape is shaded?

11 Shape A _____

12 Shape B _____

13 Shape C _____

14 Shape D _____

15 Shape E _____

B 12

Which of the shapes would fold to make a closed cube?

16 Shape _____

B 21

6

Put in the next number in each of these sequences.

17 2   6   18   _____

18 1.75   1.96   2.17   _____

19 1.5   3   6   _____

20 0.01   0.04   0.09   0.16   _____

Calculate these values.

21 $\frac{3}{5}$ of £17.35 =   _____

22 $\frac{1}{6}$ of £13.80 =   _____

23 $\frac{4}{9}$ of £2.97 =   _____

24 $\frac{5}{8}$ of £2.56 =   _____

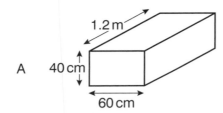
A   40 cm   1.2 m   60 cm

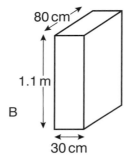
80 cm   1.1 m   B   30 cm

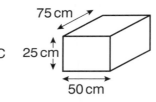
75 cm   C   25 cm   50 cm

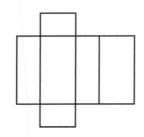

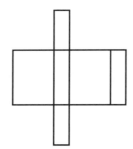

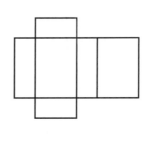

I flattened three cardboard boxes for recycling. Using the diagrams of each box and its net, work out the surface area of the three boxes. Give your answers in square metres.

25 Box A   _____

26 Box B   _____

27 Box C   _____

28–32 Put these fractions in order from smallest to largest.

$\frac{7}{12}$ $\frac{1}{2}$ $\frac{4}{6}$ $\frac{9}{16}$ $\frac{5}{8}$

_____   _____   _____   _____   _____

33–36 If the sum of the digits of a number is divisible by three then the number is divisible by three. Circle the numbers below that are divisible by 3.

261   173   405   412   506   273   369   316

37–40 Mr Jolley delivers central heating oil in our village. The price of oil is 90p per litre. Complete the table below to show how much each of four villagers paid recently to top up their oil tanks.

Customer	Capacity of tank	Fraction of oil in tank	Cost of top up
Mr Klein	280 litres	$\frac{5}{7}$ full	_____
Mrs Beattie	250 litres	$\frac{4}{5}$ full	_____
Ms Abramsen	240 litres	$\frac{3}{8}$ full	_____
Mr Dowel	270 litres	$\frac{7}{9}$ full	_____

I am about to roll a fair dice. Writing each answer in its **lowest terms**, what is the probability that I will roll:

41 a 3? _____

42 an odd number? _____

43 a number less than 5? _____

44 a 7? _____

45 a number between 0 and 7? _____

Simplify these expressions.

46 $6a + 4a - 7 + 3 =$ _____

47 $2x^2 + 5 + 3x^2 - 2 =$ _____

48 $4p + 3q - 2p - q =$ _____

49 $16z + 3y - 13z + 2y =$ _____

50 $4a^2 - 3b - 2a^2 - 4b =$ _____

Paper 21

Calculate the answers to these.

1 $7.2 + 16.5 + 0.8 =$ _____

2 $19.2 + 3.06 + 48.99 =$ _____

3 $17.93 - 8.2 =$ _____

4 $43.05 - 0.15 =$ _____ **4**

Work out the answers to these questions. Remember to calculate what is in the brackets first.

5 $(7 \times 6) - (4 \times 2) + (16 \div 2) =$ _____

6 $(6 \times 9) + 3.5 - (27 \div 3) =$ _____

7 $(7 + 3) - (5 - 2) + (5 + 2) =$ _____

8 $(36 \div 6) + (36 - 6.3) =$ _____ **4**

9–13 Put these in order from smallest to largest.

    1.25   –0.5   1.5   –0.75   –1.25

    _____   _____   _____   _____   _____ **5**

What are the missing numbers in these multiplications?

14 $2 \times 3 \times 5 \times \underline{} = 240$ **15** $4 \times 7 \times 9 \times \underline{} = 2772$

16 $11 \times 12 \times \underline{} = 1848$ **3**

Write the following numbers as products of prime **factors**.

17–20 $90 = \underline{} \times \underline{} \times \underline{} \times \underline{}$

21–22 $15 = \underline{} \times \underline{}$ **6**

23 If it takes me 44 minutes to walk 4 km, how long will it take for me to walk 10 km at the same rate? _____ h _____ min

24 6 metres of fabric costs me £24. How much will $9\frac{1}{2}$ metres cost? _____

25 If it costs me £4.95 in fuel to travel 45 km, how much will it cost for me to travel 65 km? _____ **3**

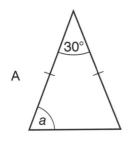

A

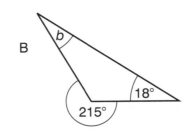

B

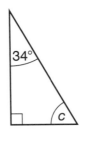

C

Name each of these triangles and calculate angles a, b and c.

26–27 Triangle A is an _____ triangle and angle *a* is _____°.

28–29 Triangle B is a _____ triangle and angle *b* is _____°.

30–31 Triangle C is a _____ triangle and angle *c* is _____°.

Metric	Imperial
550 ml	1 pint
454 g	1 pound
1600 m	1 mile

Calculate the answers using the approximate metric equivalents in this table.

32 How many litres in $6\frac{1}{2}$ pints? _____ l

33 How many kilograms in $2\frac{1}{2}$ pounds? _____ kg

34 How many kilometres in $3\frac{1}{2}$ miles? _____ km

Calculate these values.

35 $\frac{2}{3}$ of £45.81 = _____

36 $\frac{3}{5}$ of £180.75 = _____

37 $12\frac{1}{2}$% of £48 = _____

38 80% of £62.70 = _____

Find the answers to these calculations.

39 $(3 \times 1.25) - (4 \times 1.5)$ = _____

40 $(16.8 \div 4) - (7.3 + 1.6)$ = _____

41 $(21 - 18) - (21 + 18)$ = _____

B 18
B 17
6
B 25
3
B 10
B 12
4
B 3
B 2
3

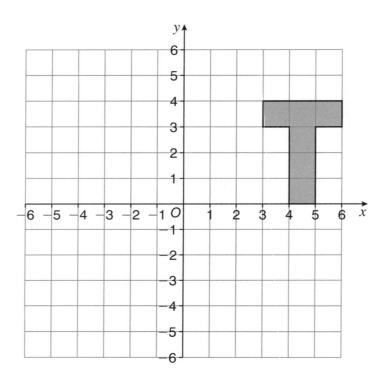

42 Translate the T shape 7 units left and 2 units up.

43 Now reflect the translated shape in the horizontal axis.

44 Finally translate the reflected shape 5 units right and 1 unit up.

Give the full name of each **polygon**.

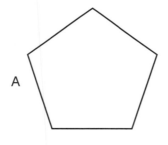
A

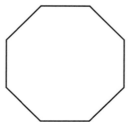
B

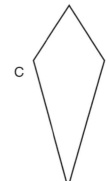
C

45 A is a _____

46 B is a _____

47 C is a _____

Calculate the volume of each cuboid.

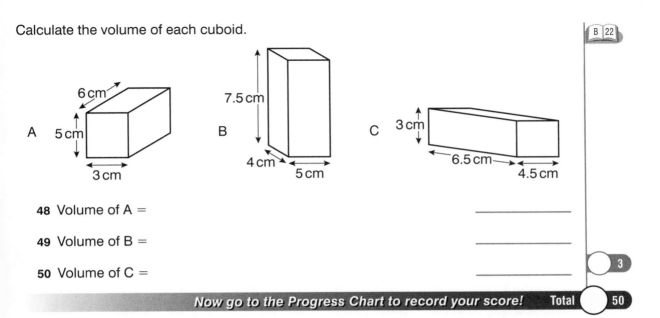

A   6 cm   5 cm   3 cm

B   7.5 cm   4 cm   5 cm

C   3 cm   6.5 cm   4.5 cm

B 22

48 Volume of A = _____

49 Volume of B = _____

50 Volume of C = _____   3

Now go to the Progress Chart to record your score!   **Total**   50

Paper 22

1 There are 28 poster spaces along each side of 12 escalators.
How many posters can be displayed?   _____ posters

B 3

2 Greeting cards come in packs of 35.
How many packs can be made from 945 cards?   _____ packs

B 3

3 What is the smallest number with six different digits not including
zero that begins with 2 and ends with 3?   _____

B 1

4 What is the greatest number with six different digits not including
zero that begins with 3 and ends with 2?   _____

B 1

5 A netball team won 70% of the games they played last season.
In total they played 20 games. How many did they lose?   _____

B 12

  5

Every card in a deck of 52 playing cards has an equal chance of being chosen. Writing
your answers as fractions in the **lowest terms**, what is the probability of choosing:

B 16

6 a black card?   _____

7 a red six?   _____

8 the ace of diamonds?   _____

9 a spade?   _____

  4

10–13 Here is the set of pentominoes. B 21

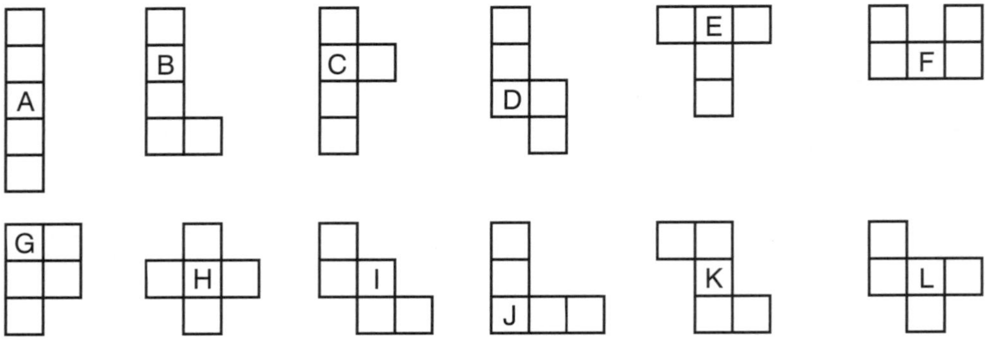

Write down the letters of those that would not fold to make an open topped cube.

____ ____ ____ ____ 4

Write the pairs of **prime numbers** between 1 and 20 that have a difference of 2. The first pair is given. B 6

3 and 5

14–15 ___ and ___

16–17 ___ and ___

18–19 ___ and ___ 6

Write the numbers of lines of symmetry in these **polygons**. B27/B18 B 19

20 Isosceles **trapezium** ____

21 Isosceles triangle ____

22 Equilateral triangle ____

23 Regular octagon ____

24 **Rhombus** ____

25 Regular pentagon ____ 6

Calculate the answers to these fraction problems, giving each answer in the **lowest terms**. B 10

26 $\frac{7}{12} - \frac{19}{36} =$ ____

27 $3\frac{3}{4} - 2\frac{5}{8} =$ ____

28 $4\frac{9}{14} + 7\frac{24}{35} =$ ____

29 $5\frac{13}{27} + 6\frac{11}{18} =$ ____

30 $2\frac{5}{6} \times 3 =$ ____ 5

5

Calculate the areas of these triangles. Each small square on the grid is 2 mm × 2 mm.

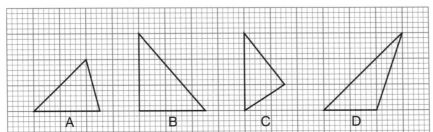

31 A has an area of _____ cm²

32 B has an area of _____ cm²

33 C has an area of _____ cm²

34 D has an area of _____ cm²

Find the values of *a*, *b* and *c*.

35 $5a + 3^2 = 24$ $a = $ _____

36 $2b^2 - 28 = 4$ $b = $ _____

37 $6^2 - 4c = 8$ $c = $ _____

Use the values that you have found for *a*, *b* and *c* to solve these.

38 $a^2 + 3b - c = $ _____

39 $ab + c = $ _____

40 $4a - 6b + 2c - 2 = $ _____

Insert one of these signs +, −, × or ÷ to make each statement correct.

41 168 ___ 14 = 12

42 168 ___ 14 = 154

43 168 ___ 14 = 182

44 168 ___ 14 = 2352

Work out the answers to these measures problems.

45 163 cm + 1050 mm + 0.2 m = _____ cm

46 15 m − 836 cm + 836 mm = _____ cm

47 1156 g + 3.8 kg = _____ kg

48 0.25 kg + 837 g = _____ kg

49 536 ml + 0.7 litres − 826 ml = _____ ml

50 1.55 litres − 1256 ml + 7 ml = _____ ml

Paper 23

Solve these decimal division problems.

B 11

1 $121.5 \div 9 =$ _____

2 $27.6 \div 6 =$ _____

3 $73.75 \div 5 =$ _____

4 $142 \div 4 =$ _____

Write in the missing numbers.

5 $35 \times 24 =$ ___ $\times 84$

6 $56 \times 9 = 36 \times$ ___

7 $7 \times 48 = 12 \times$ ___

8 $36 \times 8 =$ ___ $\times 9$

Use one of these symbols $>$, $<$ or $=$ in these statements.

9 $4^2 - 3^2$ ___ 2^3

10 $5^2 + 2^2$ ___ $20 + 3^2$

11 $48 - 6^2$ ___ $2^2 + 7$

12 $11^2 - 10^2$ ___ 5^2

13 $4^2 + 5^2 + 6^2 + 7^2$ ___ 11^2

Last summer I was given an electronic weather station. Here are the temperatures in °C that I recorded over two weeks in June.

15   17   20   20   23   19   17   16   15   19   22   20   23   20

14 What is the **mode**? _____

15 What is the **mean**? _____

16 What is the **median**? _____

17 What is the **range**? _____

18–19 Other than 1, what are the common **factors** of 18 and 27?   ___ and ___

20–21 What are the common **factors** of 32 and 44?   ___ and ___

22 If $x = 3$ and $y = 3x - 4$,   then $y =$ _____

23 If $a = 7$ and $b = a^2 - 29$,   then $b =$ _____

24 If $p = 4$ and $q = 5^2 - p^2$,   then $q =$ _____

25 If $r = 2$ and $s = r^3 - 7$,   then $s =$ _____

26–30 Put these fractions in order, least first.

$\frac{3}{8}$ $\frac{1}{16}$ $\frac{5}{7}$ $\frac{2}{7}$ $\frac{1}{32}$

___   ___   ___   ___   ___

Here is a set of three boxes and their nets.

A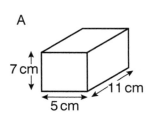

7 cm
5 cm
11 cm

B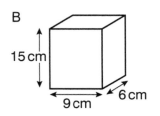

15 cm
9 cm
6 cm

C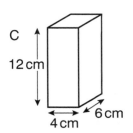

12 cm
4 cm
6 cm

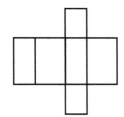
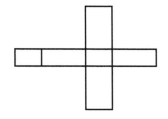
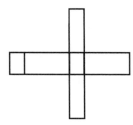

Calculate the surface area for each of the boxes.

31 The surface area of box A = _____

32 The surface area of box B = _____

33 The surface area of box C = _____

Now, calculate the perimeter of the net of each box.

34 The perimeter of net A = _____

35 The perimeter of net B = _____

36 The perimeter of net C = _____

Estimate the numbers that the arrows are indicating in each of these.

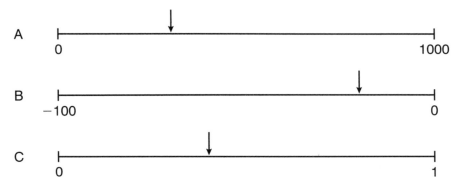

A
0   1000

B
−100   0

C
0   1

37 The arrow on line A, to the nearest 100, is pointing at _____

38 The arrow on line B, to the nearest 10, is pointing at _____

39 The arrow on line C, to the nearest 0.1, is pointing at _____

3

Approximate equivalent measurements

4.5 litres is about 1 gallon.
1 kilogram is about 2.2 pounds.
8 kilometres is about 5 miles.
30 grams is about 1 ounce.

Equivalent measurements

There are 14 pounds in a stone.
There are 16 ounces in a pound.
There are 8 pints in a gallon.

Using this information work out the answers to these problems. Round up or down as necessary.

40 My car does 45 miles per gallon. How many kilometres is that? _____ km

41 How many miles do I travel on 1 litre of fuel? _____ miles

42 I weigh 12 stone. What is that in kilograms? _____ kg

43 Using only information from the approximate column, work out how many grams are there in 1 pound. _____ g

44 How many gallons are there in 27 litres? _____ gallons

5

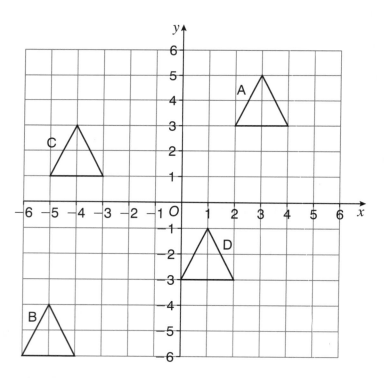

45–46 Translating the shape from A to B is _____ units left, and _____ units down.

47–48 Translating the shape from C to D is _____ units right, and _____ units down.

49–50 Translating the shape from D to A is _____ units right, and _____ units up.

6

Paper 24

1–5 Any number that has digits that sum to 9 is divisible by 9. Use this fact to circle the numbers that are divisible by 9.

289   198   609   513   396   1284   1089   2354   1170   3036

Put one of the signs $<$, $>$ or $=$ in these statements to make them correct.

6 $4^2 \times 2$ ___ $6^2 - 3$

7 $11^2 \times 3$ ___ $6^2 \times 10$

8 $2^2 \times 3^2$ ___ 6^2

9 $4^2 + 5^2$ ___ 6^2

10 $10^2 \div 5$ ___ $6^2 - 15$

11–13 Draw the reflections of these shapes in the mirror line.

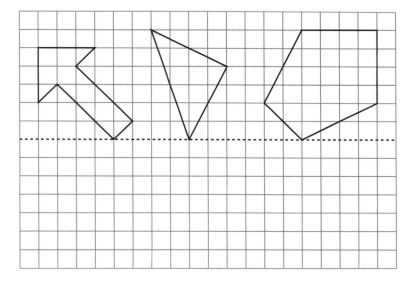

14–19 Complete this table.

Length	Breadth	Perimeter	Area
16 cm	9 cm	___ cm	___ cm²
14 cm	___ cm	44 cm	___ cm²
13 cm	___ cm	___ cm	91 cm²

69

Calculate the areas of these right-angled triangles.

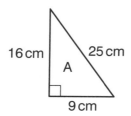

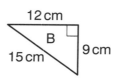

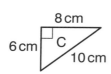

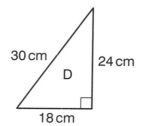

20 Triangle A = _____

21 Triangle B = _____

22 Triangle C = _____

23 Triangle D = _____

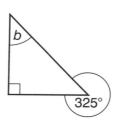

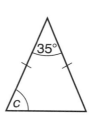

Calculate the values of the marked angles *a*, *b* and *c*.

24 Angle *a* = _____°

25 Angle *b* = _____°

26 Angle *c* = _____°

Find the answers to these multiplication problems.

27 $450 \times 18 =$ _____

28 $322 \times 14 =$ _____

29 $304 \times 16 =$ _____

30 $896 \times 28 =$ _____

31–35 On the grid below draw five different ways that four square tiles can be laid down so that each tile touches the side of another tile. None of your answers should be rotations or reflections of each other.

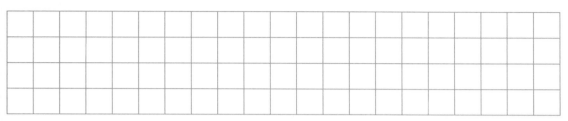

4

Calculate the values in these expressions.

36–37 A + B + C = 196   A = 82, B = 2C   B = _____ C = _____

38–39 X + Y + Z = 234   Y = 106, X = 3Z   X = _____ Z = _____

4

Find the answers to these calculations. Give your answers as whole numbers or fractions as appropriate.

40 $4\frac{1}{2} \div 1\frac{1}{2} =$ _____   **41** $1\frac{1}{2} \div 4\frac{1}{2} =$ _____

42 $\frac{1}{2} \div \frac{1}{4} =$ _____   **43** $\frac{1}{2} \div \frac{1}{3} =$ _____

4

44 How many items can I buy with £6 if each item costs 82p?   _____

45 How many items can I buy with £20 if each item costs £1.75?   _____

2

46–50 List, in order, the first five **prime numbers** greater than 2.

_____ _____ _____ _____ _____

5

Now go to the Progress Chart to record your score!   Total   50

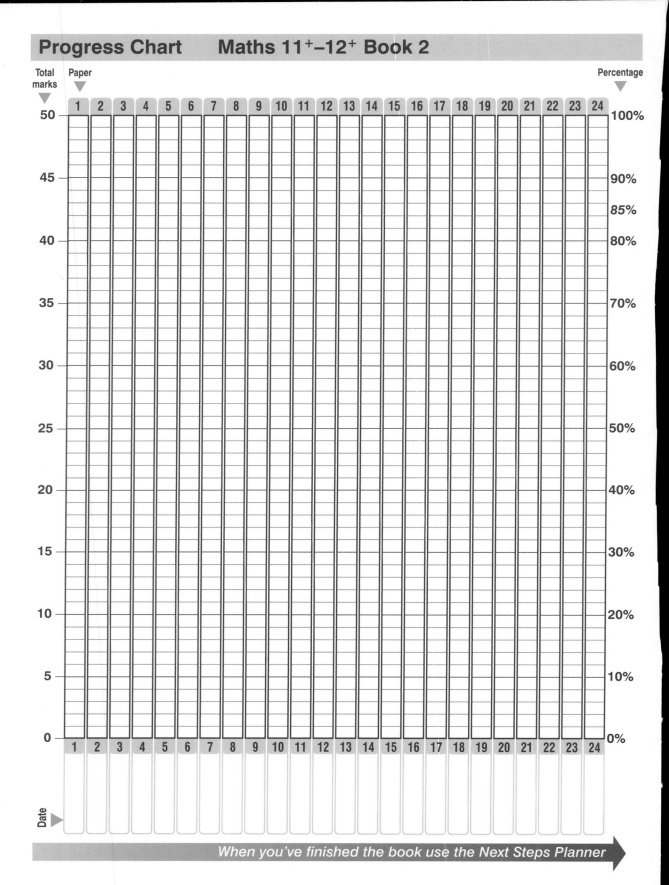